The Bible Speaks Today

Series Editors: J. A. Motyer (OT)
John R. W. Stott (NT)

The Message of Hosea
Love to the Loveless

Titles in this series

The Message of Hosea

Love to the Loveless

Derek Kidner

formerly Warden of Tyndale House, Cambridge

Inter-Varsity Press
Leicester, England
Downers Grove, Illinois, U.S.A.

InterVarsity Press
38 De Montfort Street, Leicester LE1 7GP, England
P.O. Box 1400, Downers Grove, Illinois 60515, U.S.A.

© *1981 by Derek Kidner. Originally published under the title* Love to the Loveless.

Inter-Varsity Press, England, is the book-publishing division of the Universities and Colleges Christian Fellowship (formerly the Inter-Varsity Fellowship), a student movement linking Christian Unions in universities and colleges throughout the United Kingdom and the Republic of Ireland, and a member movement of the International Fellowship of Evangelical Students. For information about local and national activities in Great Britain write to UCCF, 38 De Montfort Street, Leicester LE1 7GP.

InterVarsity Press, U.S.A., is the book-publishing division of InterVarsity Christian Fellowship, a student movement active on campus at hundreds of universities, colleges and schools of nursing. For information about local and regional activities, write Public Relations Dept., InterVarsity Christian Fellowship, 6400 Schroeder Rd., P.O. Box 7895, Madison, WI 53707-7895.

Cover photograph: Robert Cushman Hayes

UK ISBN 0-85110-730-3 (paperback)
USA ISBN 0-87784-290-6 (paperback)
USA ISBN 0-87784-925-0 (set of The Bible Speaks Today, *paperback)*

Text set in Great Britain
Printed in the United States of America ♾

Library of Congress Cataloging-in-Publication Data

Kidner, Derek.
[Love to the loveless]
The message of Hosea : love to the loveless / Derek Kidner.
p. cm. — (The Bible speaks today)
Originally published: Love to the loveless. Downers Grove, Ill.:
InterVarsity Press, ©1981.
ISBN 0-87784-290-6
1. Bible. O.T. Hosea—Commentaries. I. Title. II. Series.
BS1565.3.K44 1981
224'.6077—dc19 88-28661
CIP

21	20	19	18	17	16	15	14	13	12	11	10
10	09	08	07	06	05	04	03	02	01	00	

General preface

The Bible Speaks Today describes a series of both Old Testament and New Testament expositions, which are characterized by a threefold ideal: to expound the biblical text with accuracy, to relate it to contemporary life, and to be readable.

These books are, therefore, not 'commentaries', for the commentary seeks rather to elucidate the text than to apply it, and tends to be a work rather of reference than of literature. Nor, on the other hand, do they contain the kind of 'sermons' which attempt to be contemporary and readable, without taking Scripture seriously enough.

The contributors to this series are all united in their convictions that God still speaks through what he has spoken, and that nothing is more necessary for the life, health and growth of Christians than that they should hear what the Spirit is saying to them through his ancient—yet ever modern—Word.

J. A. MOTYER
J. R. W. STOTT
Series Editors

Contents

Addenda

Author's preface

I am glad of this chance to thank the Series Editor and the editorial staff for the trouble they have taken in seeing this book through to the light of day.

I have a slight fear that the comments on (especially) the opening chapters of Hosea may be found a little heavy-going – unlike the inspired text itself which is brilliantly alive. May I therefore suggest that a discouraged and flagging reader should turn to the 'Bird's-eye view' at the back of the book, to get his bearings and return refreshed to complete his journey with this remarkable prophet.

DEREK KIDNER

Chief abbreviations

ANET	*Ancient Near Eastern Texts* edited by J. B. Pritchard, ³1969.
AV	Authorized Version (King James'), 1611.
BDB	*Hebrew-English Lexicon of the Old Testament* by F. Brown, S. R. Driver and C. A. Briggs, 1907.
BH	*Biblia Hebraica* edited by R. Kittel and P. Kahle, ⁷1951.
BHS	*Biblia Hebraica Stuttgartensia* edited by K. Elliger and W. Rudolph, 1977.
GNB	Good News Bible (Today's English Version), 1976.
Harper	*Amos and Hosea* by W. R. Harper (*International Critical Commentary*, T. & T. Clark), 1905.
Heb.	Hebrew.
IEJ	*Israel Exploration Journal.*
JAOS	*Journal of the American Oriental Society.*
JB	The Jerusalem Bible, 1966.
JTS	*Journal of Theological Studies.*
K-B	*Lexicon in Veteris Testamenti Libros* edited by L. Koehler and W. Baumgartner, 1953.
Knight	*Hosea* by G. A. F. Knight (*Torch Bible Commentaries*, SCM Press), 1960.
LXX	The Septuagint (pre-Christian Greek Version of the Old Testament).
Mays	*Hosea* by J. L. Mays (*Old Testament Library*, SCM Press), 1969.

mg.	margin.
MT	Massoretic Text (standard text of the Hebrew Bible).
NEB	The New English Bible, Old Testament, 1970.
NIV	New International Version, 1979.
Pusey	*The Minor Prophets* by E. B. Pusey, 1879.
RSV	American Revised Standard Version, 1952.
RV	English Revised Version, 1881.
Smith	*The Book of the Twelve Prophets* by George Adam Smith (*The Expositor's Bible*) 1, [7]1900.
Syr.	The Peshitta (Syriac Version of the Bible).
VT	*Vetus Testamentum.*
Wolff	*Hosea* by H. W. Wolff (*Biblischer Kommentar* XIV, [2]1965); English translation by G. Stansell (Fortress Press), 1974.

To the reader . . .

It is rather easy to grow up with a naïve idea of God – something like a child's impression of the adult world – and with a worrying conundrum about His way of doing things. The conundrum is this old one: If God is all-powerful and all-good, why does He not rid the world of evil? (The church too, for that matter?)

One of the things that Hosea does for us is to give us, with extraordinary frankness, the other side of that anomaly. God's side.

The child's idea of his elders is a puzzled one. *They* make the rules (he says to himself) – there's power for you! And they have money, whatever they may say – there's freedom! What couldn't we do, we children, with all that freedom, all that power?

In this book we see things not in these simplistic terms, where situations and people are uncomplicated and power is like a magic wand. Hosea introduces us to a family which is a miniature of our world – or rather, of the most enlightened part of the world of his own day. But it is a problem family, and God compares His situation not to that of an autocrat whose orders nobody dares question, nor of a father who rejoices in an adoring wife and children, but to that of a husband whose wife has left him, and a father whose children are like strangers in his own house and are fast destroying themselves.

Where does omnipotence, where do instant solutions come into such a picture? Certainly tame acceptance is no answer to it, but no more are strong-arm tactics – unless one were content to have a slave-wife, and a family simply cowed into conformity.

With relationships as subtle and sensitive as these, there are no short cuts to mending them when they go wrong; not even for omnipotence. (If we think that God could somehow wave that wand and solve the problem painlessly if He really gave His mind to it, we have only to recall the cross, that hideous instrument of torture, and the Son's prayer, 'My Father, *if it be possible ...*',[1] for our answer.)

But all this may seem somewhat theoretical and remote. So God brought it home to Hosea, at ground level and at painful length, by telling him to do the last thing a responsible prophet might expect. '*Go and marry a prostitute* – because' (if we may paraphrase it this way) 'this is exactly what I, the Lord, have married in pledging myself to all of *you.*'

And Hosea did not gather that he could simply go through a form of marriage, or alternatively that God would find him a prostitute with a heart of gold. He married a shallow, mercenary woman, the kind who might walk out on him the moment it suited her; and they started a family.

She bore him a son. After that, she had two more children, who were apparently not his. Then she left him.

She had made a fool of him; she had also made a fool of herself, for her new lover turned out to be as useless and heartless as herself, and she was soon his drudge and virtual prisoner. It was rather like the plight of the Prodigal Son.

But the story does not end in quite the same way as the well-known parable. In a sense it surpasses it. She makes no move (perhaps none is possible) to come home. It is Hosea, her husband, who goes to find her; and when he does, he not only has to win her back but buy her back, scraping together the price partly in cash and partly in kind. And more: it is not just an act of re-possession, for God had said to him, 'Go again and *love* a woman loved by another man, an adulteress, and *love her as I, the Lord, love* the Israelites although they resort to other gods.'[2]

There is precious little exercise of power in such a story of the 'eternal triangle', for power alone would solve nothing. Instead, there is hurt, humiliation, waiting, personal approach and appeal, and, at last, mutual commitment. Cost, too; but mostly the cost of risking rebuff, reopening wounds, working

---

[1] Mt. 26:39, 42, 44.   [2] Ho. 3:1, NEB (my italics).

at a difficult relationship and being determined that it shall last and grow. 'I will allure her,' says God, '... and speak tenderly to her. ... And I will betroth you to me for ever.'[3] And Hosea, for his part, says to his wife Gomer that he is not for sharing, nor is she. 'You must dwell as mine for many days; you shall not play the harlot. or belong to another man; so will I also be to you.'[4]

That is the story of the first three chapters. But when God draws out the large-scale meaning of it, it turns out that the pattern of relationships, between Him, His people and His rivals for their affection, is not so much a triangle as a veritable polygon. In every direction His people have played Him false:
  – in religion, with other gods, another cult;
  – in politics, with shabby intrigues and dubious patrons;
  – in morals, with unbridled sex and violence.
His reaction might well have been to write them off and waste no more affection on them. But He is not so easily dismissed.

So far, I have been playing down the role of forceful intervention. But it would be a gross distortion of this book to make it portray God as simply wringing His hands. There is anger here, and judgment; it is not all pleading. At this point it may help us to see the realities of the situation and the lack of easy remedies, if we glance at the troubles of our own society and the simplistic cures that are proposed for them. 'Play it cool', one school of thought will urge the legislators: let the facts of life bring people to their senses in their own time. 'Play it tough' will be another view: bring in stiffer laws and savage penalties. 'Play it tenderly' will be a third opinion: appeal to people's better feelings; trust the strong to act with moderation.

Each of these *by itself* would cut a vital corner, to leave an open path to either anarchy or civil war or a bullies' paradise. One must have, it seems, the right mix of all three of them, or more; a complex answer to a complex situation.

In Hosea, God is by turns '*cool*' ('he has withdrawn from them'; 'Ephraim is joined to idols, let him alone'; 'They sow the wind, and they shall reap the whirlwind'[5]) and '*tough*' ('I will be like a lion to Ephraim'; 'he will remember their iniquity, he will punish their sins'[6]); but above all, '*tender*' ('How can I give you

---

[3] Ho. 2:14, 19.   [4] Ho. 3:3.   [5] Ho. 5:6; 4:17; 8:7.
[6] Ho. 5:14; 9:9.

up, O Ephraim! . . . My heart recoils within me . . .'; 'I will heal their faithlessness . . .'[7]).

And Israel? She got it wrong, in the usual human way. God, she reckoned, must be wanting more religion; she would bring more sacrifices. 'They love sacrifice', says God. 'With their flocks and herds they shall go to seek the Lord.'[8] But that was not the way to find Him. These were religious *things*, and He wanted people: converted people, deeply repentant, wholly and for ever His. All the ups and downs of the book, the scathing portraits, dire predictions, ardent appeals, add up to this; and the book ends by looking to the fruit of all this agony, when this unequal marriage, like Hosea's, will be no longer full of tensions and betrayals, but secure and blissful, its long winter over and its spring at last arrived and in full flower.

What, then, has this prophet to say to us today? This at least:
- that God is not the distant magician of our childish imagining (which is where we began), but one who works within the very limits and freedoms that can make or break a marriage, a family, a people or a person;
- that He loves the loveless, and values the otherwise worthless – enough to let the ransom for them cost Him everything;[9]
- but equally, that He will never be content to form one side of any triangle – still less, of any polygon! – or to be the bridegroom of a day or two. He will settle for nothing less than love, nothing shorter than 'for ever'.

So, 'whoever is wise',[10] 'take with you words, and turn to the Lord', perhaps in the very language of 14:2–3 (here quoted from the AV):

> say unto him,
> 'Take away all iniquity,
> and receive us graciously:
> . . . for in thee the fatherless findeth mercy.'

Then we can expect to hear from Him the princely response which words from the heart, such as these, will still evoke:

---

[7] Ho. 11:8; 14:4. [8] Ho. 8:13; 5:6.

[9] See the comments, below, on 3:2 and 13:14.

[10] This is how the epilogue, the last verse of the book, addresses us. It is not a message simply for its own times or its first hearers.

> 'I will heal their backsliding,
> I will love them freely:
> for mine anger is turned away . . .'

And the poetry that follows this, although it speaks to ancient Israel, still speaks volumes to us as the dry, drab and superficial creatures that we are:

> 'I will be as the dew unto Israel:
> he shall grow as the lily,
> and cast forth his roots as Lebanon.'

Such is the God who meets us, exposes us, wrestles with us, and, if we will, heals us in these chapters.

Part One: a parable from life
A DISTRACTED FAMILY
Hosea 1–3

It is the people you love who can hurt you most. One can almost trace the degree of potential pain along a scale – from the rebuff which you hardly notice from a stranger, to the rather upsetting clash you may have with a friend, right on to the stinging hurt of a jilting, the ache of a parent-child estrangement, or, most wounding of all, the betrayal of a marriage.

Nothing short of the last two of these could really have conveyed to Hosea or to us how deeply God cares about us. Even then, words alone might have failed to bring home the sharpness of it. It needed acting out, and in real life at that.

After the briefest of time-notes, in the opening verse, we are plunged straight into the story.

Introducing Hosea

1:1 *The word of the Lord that came to Hosea the son of Beeri, in the days of Uzziah, Jotham, Ahaz, and Hezekiah, kings of Judah, and in the days of Jeroboam the son of Joash, king of Israel.*

So we make acquaintance with the prophet and his times. His name has suffered a little in its journey into English via Greek and Latin (where it is called Osee), for it should be Hoshea – the name also of the last king of Israel (2 Ki. 17:1), and the name originally borne by Joshua. Like Joshua/Jesus, it is derived from the verb 'to save'.[1]

---

[1] See Nu. 13:8 (Hoshea) with 14:6 (Joshua) = Ne. 8:17 (Jeshua) = Acts 7:45, AV (Jesus). 'Jesus' is the Greek form of Jeshua/Joshua.

The kings who are named here span most of the 8th century BC, but they are outshone by the brilliant prophets of that time: Jonah, Amos and Hosea in (mainly) the north, and Micah and Isaiah in the south.[2]

It had been at first a time of growing affluence, thanks to the brief respite which these little kingdoms found themselves enjoying while their strongest neighbours happened, for once, to be preoccupied and weak. Damascus, their most recent scourge, had been crippled by Assyria in 802; and then Assyria itself, that grim Mesopotamian war-machine, had begun to falter under threats from without and disunity within.

But with Israel's wealth had come increasing decadence; and then, halfway through the century, their world began to crumble. At home, the two strong kings, Jeroboam II of Israel and his contemporary, Uzziah of Judah, were at or near the end of their long reigns, while in the distance Assyria had roused itself to a new pitch of terrifying strength and militancy. It was soon to march on Palestine. Within a generation the kingdom of Israel would be extinct.

It was to this generation that Hosea was sent to preach repentance.

Hosea 1:2–9
An ominous beginning

1:2 *When the Lord first spoke through Hosea, the Lord said to Hosea, 'Go, take to yourself a wife of harlotry and have children of harlotry, for the land commits great harlotry by forsaking the Lord.'* *3aSo he went and took Gomer the daughter of Diblaim...*

A prophet's call could be agonizing: he would know that almost anything might be asked of him. It would be hard,

---

[2] North and south had split apart in the 10th century BC after the death of Solomon, to form two kingdoms, existing mostly at odds with one another. The ten tribes of the north ('Israel', or 'Ephraim') had a turbulent history of coups and counter-coups, and were more exposed than the small southern kingdom ('Judah') to invasion. Judah was ruled, throughout, by a single dynasty, the house of David. For details, see the table on pp. 130ff. and the map on p. 129. The fact that Hosea mentions here no northern king after Jeroboam may indicate that, like Amos (Am. 7:12f.), he was forced to prophesy to Israel from the safety of the land of Judah in his later years.

though, to find a more shattering first demand than was made of Hosea. The Jerusalem Bible (JB) gives it to us with almost the merciless brevity of the original: 'Go, marry a whore, and get children with a whore, for the country itself has become nothing but a whore by abandoning Yahweh.'

This is strong talk. And as if throwing the word 'whore' at us three times in one sentence were not enough, the Hebrew has the root not a mere three times, but four.[3]

Was it meant literally?

On the face of it, yes: exactly as it reads. Possibly, though, it may foreshorten the picture, leaping ahead to what this woman would become, as God could see. (This way of taking it is not as arbitrary as it may look, since this is evidently how the children are mentioned. They were future, as the unfolding story shows, yet the command of verse 2 runs literally 'take to yourself a wife of harlotry and children of harlotry', as though the latter already existed.)

The harsher view, that Gomer was a whore already, seems to me the right one; but whichever view we take, we should not soften it by making her a cult-prostitute, merely deluded and misused; for the Hebrew has a word for this (4:14), and it is not the word used here.[4] What Hosea had to do was, in miniature, what God had done in giving His love to a partner with a history and with a roving eye. Hosea was not to leave the matter there, any more than God would; but that belongs to a later part of the story, told in chapter 3.

Meanwhile, in this opening phase, it is the children who must capture our attention. What they are and what they are called will be the embodiment of God's word to Israel and to us: each of them a living sign and portent.

The first portent: the boy Jezreel

1:3b *And she conceived and bore him a son. [4] And the Lord said*

---

[3] The expression 'has become nothing but a whore' (JB), or 'commits great harlotry' (RSV), renders a Hebrew construction which uses the verbal root twice over (infinitive absolute plus imperfect) – a common way of reinforcing a statement.

[4] Still less should we allegorize it away. While the children's names were given them to convey a message, the name Gomer and her father's name Diblaim are marks of actuality, as are the statements concerning each child's conception and birth.

to him, 'Call his name Jezreel; for yet a little while, and I will punish the house of Jehu for the blood of Jezreel, and I will put an end to the kingdom of the house of Israel.' And on that day, I will break the bow of Israel in the valley of Jezreel.'

The three portents are a crescendo – first of judgment, but in the end a crescendo of grace to round off each of the first two chapters. Grace has a way of interrupting oracles of doom (like the 'cheerfulness' which 'was always breaking in' when Dr Johnson's friend began philosophizing[5]); but for the moment there is no break in the clouds, and the darkness will get deeper with each successive birth.

Jezreel (yizr'el) might not seem to be a particularly ominous name. In its form it was the same type of name as Israel *(yiśrā'ēl)*, and although it could yield a hidden meaning, to be brought out in 2:23 (see pp. 38f.), it would speak in the first place of a well-known town and valley of the northern kingdom. That town, though, had seen King Jehu's bloodbath,[6] and God is showing that He has not for a moment forgotten this. For a prophet to give his son such a name was like a politician naming his child Peterloo or Katyn or Soweto. And he would miss no opportunity of explaining it.

The explanation in verse 4, which foretells retribution on the house of Jehu, goes on to include the whole kingdom; and so in fact it came about. The house of Jehu fell in about 752 BC with King Zechariah's murder (2 Ki. 15:8–12), and after thirty years of coups and counter-coups the kingdom was torn to pieces by Assyria, never to recover.

There is a paradox over Jehu. Here he is a man of blood, storing up disaster for his dynasty and realm; but in 2 Kings 10:30 he has 'done well' in carrying out against the house of Ahab 'all that was in (God's) heart'. The reason is not far to seek; it lies in Jehu himself, a standing example of a human scourge. As God's executioner he left nothing undone, and it was in that capacity that he collected his reward: the promise of the throne to four generations of his sons. The Old Testament has several instances of this kind of servant, of whom Sennacherib, whom God calls 'the rod of my anger' ('But he does not

---

[5] *Boswell's Life of Johnson* (Everyman), II, p. 218.
[6] The gruesome story is told in 2 Ki. 9 and 10. For Jehu's place among the kings of Israel, see the table of kings on p. 130.

so intend, and his mind does not so think', Is. 10:7), and Nebuchadnezzar 'my servant' (Je. 27:6) are prime examples. And they were paid their wages – paid in spoil and conquest, described in exactly these terms of 'wages' in Ezekiel 29:18–20; but paid also with the due requital of their pride and cruelty.[7]

So it was with Jehu – with the difference that he knew of his commission from the Lord. But there was no difference of spirit or method. The events of 2 Kings 10 are a welter of trickery, butchery and hypocrisy, in which the only trace of a religious motive is fanaticism – and even this is suspect in view of Jehu's charade of sacrificing to Baal (2 Ki. 10:25). Self-interest and bloodlust were his dominant springs of conduct, and it was this that made 'the blood of Jezreel' an accusing stain.

If we ask why Israel, a hundred years later, should have to suffer for this, the later chapters of the book will reply that neither Israel nor her royal house ever repudiated this attitude to violence. Jezreel was only one episode of a continuous story,[8] and God could be no party to it.

There is a double sting in the tail of this brief oracle. Usually when God promises to 'break the bow' of some fighting force, it means that He is coming to His people's rescue. There is a notable example in 2:18, and another in Psalm 46:9. But here, pointedly, it is the bow of *Israel* that He will break. As a kingdom, it is no longer a force for God, if it ever has been. To keep it intact would be an unreality. The further sting of this final sentence is the great reversal it implies by the scene of the defeat. Jezreel, the valley of Gideon's victory,[9] had been a name once covered with glory. Now, since the massacres, it could only stand for savagery.

So it turned out. In 733, a decade before the death of the kingdom as a whole, an Assyrian army fought its way into this valley and lopped off the northern territories of Israel, marching their inhabitants off to Assyria. 2 Kings 15:29 lists among these conquests 'Gilead, and Galilee'. God had broken the bow of Israel, and it lay defenceless.[10]

The second portent: the girl 'Not-Pitied'

1:6 *She conceived again and bore a daughter. And the Lord said*

[7] See, *e.g.*, Is. 10:12, 15ff.; Is. 47; Dn. 4. [8] *Cf.*, *e.g.*, 4:1–3; 7:1–7.
[9] Jdg. 6:33–7:23. [10] See the map on p. 129.

*to him, 'Call her name Not pitied, for I will no more have pity on
the house of Israel, to forgive them at all. [7]But I will have pity on
the house of Judah, and I will deliver them by the Lord their
God; I will not deliver them by bow, nor by sword, nor by war,
nor by horses, nor by horsemen.'*

The first child had been Hosea's own: his wife 'bore him a son'
(3). The second and third are not said to have been his: the 'him'
of verse 3 is missing in verses 6 and 8. So the joy of fatherhood
was deeply clouded, and the children were living proofs of the
invasion of the marriage.

The name Lo-ruhamah, '*Not pitied*', uses the same verb (but a
different part of it [11]) as in the well-known saying of Isaiah 49:15,
'Can a woman forget her sucking child, *that she should have no
compassion . . .*?' The effect of the name is startling and tragic: the
sign cuts deeper than the first one, Jezreel, for while it is shattering enough to lose a war and a kingdom, it is still more desperate
to lose the mercy and compassion of God. We must not press the
distinction too far, for this book above all reveals the persistence
of God's compassion, even in this opening chapter and still more
towards the closing pages (see especially chapter 11). But His
love is not blind, nor is it coercive. It follows that since mercy
without response is self-defeating, and forgiveness without a
healed relationship is empty, there may come a point at which
the only thing left for even God to say is, 'How often would I . .
and you would not! Behold, your house is forsaken.'[12]

The verse about Judah (7) underlines the fact that, in this
context, pity or the lack of it means not a state of mind but a
course of action, sparing or unsparing. God's *pity on the house of
Judah* would take the form of a miraculous deliverance, the
rescue of Jerusalem after Hezekiah had spread the Assyrian
ultimatum before the Lord (Is. 37:14, 33ff.).[13] There would be
no such reprieve for an impenitent Samaria.[14] Pity in that form
would only prolong the process of its dying.

[11] Strictly speaking, the name is a statement, 'She has not received compassion'. *Cf.* 2:1 (3, Heb.); 1 Pet. 2:10.

[12] Mt. 23:37f.

[13] Those who cannot entertain the idea of prediction treat verse 7 as an
insertion after the event. But it has an important function in the oracle as a
provocative challenge to Israel. 'This', God says in effect, 'is the salvation in store
for your sister-kingdom. This is what your impenitence is forfeiting.'

[14] See the information on p. 129.

It needs to be said, as well, that oracles like these are shouts of warning, not irrevocable sentences. The classic illustrations of this fact are found in Jonah and Jeremiah. Jonah's oracle, 'Yet forty days, and Nineveh shall be overthrown', was as doom-laden as even he could wish; yet he knew that it was given to avert the very judgment it foretold. Jeremiah had the principle spelt out to him in the potter's workshop, as he saw the crafts-man's response, radical and creative, to the way his material responded or failed to respond to him. God's comment was far-reaching: 'If at any time I declare concerning a nation ... that I will pluck up and break down and destroy it, (then) if that nation ... turns from its evil, I will repent of the evil that I intended to do to it' (Je. 18:7f.). This principle of all prophecy (note the words, 'at any time') throws its own light on the way the chapter will end. But before that there is worse to come.

The third portent: the boy 'Not-My-People'

1:8 *When she had weaned Not pitied, she conceived and bore a son. ⁹And the Lord said, 'Call his name Not my people, for you are not my people and I am not your God.'*

This son, Lo-ammi, like his sister (see on verse 6), seems to have been a product of Gomer's 'harlotry', as verse 2 puts it. Whether spoken or unspoken, the words 'you are not my child' must have formed themselves in the mind many times as Hosea contemplated the boy. To him as to us, the pathos of his situation could hardly fail to sensitize him to the profound sadness of the words to Israel: 'You are not my people and I am not your God'[15] – words which might otherwise have sounded only unfeeling and dismissive.

From one angle this oracle was simply factual: just as accurate as would have been Hosea's disclaimer of paternity for his children. Israel might be nominally the Lord's, but in fact she was the child of her times and of her pagan world. Likewise Yahweh might be nominally her national God; but since He is not for sharing, the presence of other gods flatly denied the relationship.

---

[15] More accurately, 'and I am not yours'. The wording of the Heb. may be meant to recall the 'I AM' passage of Ex. 3 by the contrast to Ex. 3:12, 'But I am (or, will be) with you.'

Hosea 1:10 – 2:1
A rift in the clouds

1:10 *Yet the number of the people of Israel shall be like the sand of the sea, which can be neither measured nor numbered; and in the place where it was said to them, 'You are not my people,' it shall be said to them, 'Sons of the living God.' [11]And the people of Judah and the people of Israel shall be gathered together, and they shall appoint for themselves one head; and they shall go up from the land, for great shall be the day of Jezreel.*

2:1 Say to your brother, 'My people,' and to your sister, 'She has obtained pity.'

This is astounding. Here are three disastrous oracles utterly reversed, and a promise of family reunion thrown in for good measure. But the about-turn will in fact be Israel's, not God's. The mention of 'the sand of the sea, which can be neither measured nor numbered', takes us back to Abraham, to remind us that the ancient promise is still there, and God still holds to it. One way or another – and the New Testament has surprises in store about this – He will see it through into reality.

Two of the many statements of this old promise are in fact alluded to in verse 10 (Gn. 22:17; 13:16, respectively), for God reiterated it to Abraham, and varied the analogy by speaking of stars, sand and the dust of the earth to make the matter vivid. Isaiah would have to strike a warning note about this multitude, to show that something more than simple population-growth was meant: that first there must be a sifting that would leave the merest remnant of true converts (Is. 10:20–23). Hosea has already spoken of this coming ordeal, and it forms the background to the promise.

The heart of this good news is reconciliation. The 'great … day of Jezreel' (1:11) must await explanation till 2:21f., but the giving of new names (2:1) by an act of pure grace (like that of the Christian gospel) exactly cancels the existing alienation;[1] and the warmth of 1:10b has already gone still further,

---

[1] In 2:1 (3, Heb.), the Heb. text has the plural, 'your brothers . . . your sisters'. By attaching the plural ending (here the letter *m*) to the beginning of the words that follow these, one can get near to the singular (brother . . . sister) which RSV adopts from LXX; but the plural is just as likely to be right, since the oracle is meant for all who constitute the people of Israel.

exchanging terms of covenant for those of the family: '*Sons* of the living God.' The mood is that of the great parable, as though to say, 'These my sons were dead, and are alive again; they were lost, and are found.'[2]

In terms of Old Testament Israel, the natural context is the coming exile and scattering, implied by the reversal in verse 11 when this speaks of their being gathered together and going up from the land (presumably of their captivity[3]). The other abnormality in their situation was their long-standing breach with Judah (11); and this too would be ended.

There was some degree of fulfilment of these things at the literal level – but only some. The northern kingdom ('Israel' or 'Ephraim', as distinct from Judah) never regained its cohesion after 722 BC when it was crushed and scattered. But remnants of it took refuge with Judah, and although King Hezekiah's overtures to the northern tribes were scorned at first, we read of elements from at least five of them which joined him at Jerusalem for his great Passover (2 Ch. 30:11, 18). The concept of a single people of God was far from dead. In the next century King Josiah of Judah reckoned to include the whole land of Israel in his reforms (2 Ch. 34:6–7, 9; *cf.* 35:18); and after the exile we read of people from Ephraim and Manasseh (1 Ch. 9:3) – which may be a term for the northern tribes in general – settling in Jerusalem with the men of Judah, Benjamin and Levi, the tribes which from then on formed the main body of Israel. Although 'Judah' and 'Jews' became their national name, the title that still meant most to them was 'Israel', whose tradition of twelve tribes now stood for the chosen nation in its completeness rather than its diversity.

So Ezra and his band of pilgrims from Babylonia offered 'twelve bulls for all Israel' when they reached Jerusalem (Ezr. 8:35); and Paul, long after, spoke to Agrippa of 'our twelve tribes' waiting for the hope of Israel (Acts 26:7) – to take just one New Testament example. At this level, then, the old breach between south and north had long been healed by New Testament times, though hardly in the way that might have been foreseen, and not without new roots of bitterness in the hatred between Jews and Samaritans.

[2] *Cf.* Lk. 15:24.
[3] It has been suggested that 'land' is a scribal error for 'lands'. This would make good sense and agree with other prophecies (*e.g.* Je. 16:15), but it lacks textual support and must remain a conjecture.

But we are not allowed to stop there. Twice the New Testament picks up this prophecy and turns it to face a still larger multitude, to include now Samaritans and Gentiles, to whom God was saying with even better reason:

> 'Those who were not my people
> I will call "my people",
> and her who was not beloved
> I will call "my beloved".'[4]

And this was no afterthought. As Paul reminds us, it was part of the basic promise to Abraham. 'The scripture,' he points out, 'foreseeing that God would justify the Gentiles by faith, preached the gospel beforehand to Abraham, saying, "In you shall all the nations be blessed." So then,' he adds, 'those who are men of faith are blessed with Abraham who had faith' (Gal. 3:8f.; *cf.* Rom. 4:9–25).

The prophecy, in fact, after touching-down in the post-exilic age, leaps into the present and names us who are believers 'the Israel of God', whether we are Jews or Gentiles. Such is the New Testament's unfolding of the oracle; and such a consummation was the joy that drew Jesus to the cross, 'to die ... not for the nation only, but to gather into one' (*cf.* our verse 11) 'the children of God who are scattered abroad' (Jn. 11:52).

Hosea 2:2–23
The lovers and the Lover

The delightful ending of chapter 1 was totally unexpected, the surprise of it highlighting the sheer grace of God which it reveals. Now in chapter 2 we move to the same climax, with an ending that is richly happy; but we see the divine Lover taking His time and using every art to win a response that will make the reconciliation genuine.

She is not for sharing

2:2 *'Plead with your mother, plead –*
for she is not my wife,

---

[4] See Rom. 9:25f.; *cf.* 1 Pet. 2:10f.

> *and I am not her husband –*
> *that she put away her harlotry from her face,*
> *and her adultery from between her breasts;*
> 3 *lest I strip her naked*
> *and make her as in the day she was born,*
> *and make her like a wilderness,*
> *and set her like a parched land,*
> *and slay her with thirst.*
> 4 *Upon her children also I will have no pity,*
> *because they are children of harlotry.'*

The focus shifts now from the children to the mother, and for a little while the whole distracted family is in view together. But as materials for God's analogy they will mostly have to play their separate parts. From one angle, Israel in her apostasy could be compared to a brood of children out of control (Jezreel, 1:4) or born out of wedlock (1:6–9), but from another angle Israel is like a fickle wife. The second of these will be the main theme of our chapter; but at its beginning and end the children make a brief but memorable appearance. Insofar as they stand for a separate entity within Israel, they are perhaps the actual hearers over against the corporate Israel whose history has made them what they are. Note the plurals in 2:1 (margin), and see the footnote on page 24.

We can get a slightly false impression from the opening cry, 'Plead ... plead', for it means the kind of pleading or contending that belongs to a court of law. So NEB puts it well with 'Plead my cause'. It is in fact essentially the same word as in 4:1 where the Lord has 'a controversy' with the inhabitants of the land. NEB may well be right, too, in framing the next two lines as a question: 'Is she not my wife and I her husband?' – for the whole thrust of the book is that God will not go back on the marriage vows He has exchanged with her.[1] If not a question, it must be taken existentially, to mean 'She is no longer a wife to me...' (GNB) – *i.e.*, 'the reality has gone out of the relationship'.

---

[1] There is a similar scouting of such a thought in Is. 50:1, where God treats the idea of divorce as no less preposterous than the notion that He might have had to sell her to pay His bills! He goes on to say that Israel did have to be 'sold' and 'sent away' (*i.e.*, into exile) for her sins; but He has already made it clear that this was, in C. R. North's phrase, 'separation, not divorce'.

Now, still in verse 2, comes the first of many calls to radical repentance – for it will keep emerging that Israel, like most of us, is readier to say she is sorry than to make a clean break with her way of life. And with the next two verses (3–4) comes the sharp reminder that this deserted husband is no pathetic cuckold but very much a person to be reckoned with. There is poetic justice in the threat to 'strip her naked', for it is in one sense a saturation-dose of her own medicine, cheapening her, as in verse 10, even beyond her own self-cheapening; and in another sense it speaks of stark destitution – as the desert scene of verse 3b makes plain. Hosea's own wife was to know something of both these things, degradation and want; but God is talking about Israel and her spiritual adultery, her godless progeny (verse 4, taking us back to chapter 1:6) and her coming devastation.

The rude awakening

2:5   *'For their mother has played the harlot;*
        she that conceived them has acted shamefully.
    For she said, "I will go after my lovers,
        who give me my bread and my water,
        my wool and my flax, my oil and my drink."
  6 *Therefore I will hedge up her way with thorns;*
        and I will build a wall against her,
        so that she cannot find her paths.
  7 *She shall pursue her lovers,*
        but not overtake them;
    and she shall seek them,
        but shall not find them.
    Then she shall say, "I will go
        and return to my first husband,
        for it was better with me then than now."
  8 *And she did not know*
        that it was I who gave her
        the grain, the wine, and the oil,
    and who lavished upon her silver
        and gold which they used for Baal.
  9 *Therefore I will take back*
        my grain in its time,
        and my wine in its season;

> *and I will take away my wool and my flax,*
> *which were to cover her nakedness.*
> 10 *Now I will uncover her lewdness*
> *in the sight of her lovers,*
> *and no one shall rescue her out of my hand.*
> 11 *And I will put an end to all her mirth,*
> *her feasts, her new moons, her sabbaths,*
> *and all her appointed feasts.*
> 12 *And I will lay waste her vines and her fig trees,*
> *of which she said,*
> *"These are my hire,*
> *which my lovers have given me."*
> *I will make them a forest,*
> *and the beasts of the field shall devour them.*
> 13 *And I will punish her for the feast days of the Baals*
> *when she burned incense to them*
> *and decked herself with her ring and jewelry,*
> *and went after her lovers,*
> *and forgot me, says the Lord.'*

Sexual lust can be glamourized – almost canonized – by any number of attractive names, but not everyone cares to be known for setting a price on their favours. This particular charmer is allowed no aura of romanticism. She has 'played the harlot' (5), for a harlot's 'hire' (12). Her lovers are many but her motive is one – the reward she can earn. The bulk of this chapter therefore deals with her on this level, only coming to anything deeper towards the end.

In this way as in others it has common ground with the story of the prodigal son, who came home not for love but because (as our verse 7 puts it) 'it was better with me then than now'. The love – at least initially – was all on the other side.

The prosaic facts behind the poetry of verse 5 (which would have been self-evident to those who heard it first) are that the gods of Canaan were largely patrons of fertility. To get the best results of farming one would be tempted to enlist their help, imagining that Yahweh must be somewhat out of His depth in such a realm. ('And she did not know', the Lord exclaims, 'that it was I who gave her the grain, the wine, and the oil . . .', verse 8.) More than that, these gods were Baals, meaning lords or husbands, and while some of their rituals were a re-enacting of their wars and victories, or of vegetation's death and resurrection, which would supposedly ensure the progress of the seasons and the crops, other rituals were sexual acts with cultic prostitutes, whereby the coitus at the sanctuary would magically induce fertility in the flocks and herds and farm-produce.

These beliefs and half-beliefs are not as foreign or remote from our age as they may seem. The idea that the Lord God has little relevance to the natural world is taken for granted by our secularized majority, and can be a hidden influence on even the minority who would consciously reject it. Whether His place is taken by a rational construct such as 'nature' or by the fantasies of astrology or by recourse to the occult and the demonic, it amounts to a modern dethroning of God which is hardly different from His displacement by the Baals. And this is not the only similarity between our age and theirs. If sex was deified in polytheistic thought, it receives almost equal adulation in our own. The crude pagan symbols of fertility, the likening of El or Baal to a bull,[2] the sexual acts at the sanctuary, these were not pointless pornography but expressions of a belief that this kind of potency and fecundity is what life and the world itself are chiefly about. But with it there was the fascination of the forbidden and decadent – the exciting exchange of Yahweh's broad daylight for the twilight world of violent gods, with their raw passions, cruelties and ecstasies; an exchange which has a perennial appeal.

We can note a further link with the present in the trend of Israel towards religious syncretism (that is, the mixing and merging of one religion with another); but this will be discussed in the comments on verses 16 and 17.

Returning to the text of verses 5–13 we find God speeding the process of disillusion – for such it is. The 'lovers', the pagan gods and their equivalents, are illusions that recede with every step one takes towards them; but in times of plenty this unreality is not very evident. It takes the 'thorns' and the blank 'wall' (6) of famine and frustration to dash one's hopes of them. ('Where are your gods that you made for yourself? Let them arise, if they can save you.'[3]) Even then one may not come to one's senses like the prodigal or like the truant wife who is

---

[2] *E.g.* in *ANET*, pp. 139a, 142, where the emphasis is on sexual prowess.

[3] Je. 2:28. The chapter in Jeremiah develops the theme of the unfaithful wife with considerable poetic resource.

hopefully depicted in verse 7b, but curse God like the people of Isaiah 8:21.

How wilful was Israel's ignorance (8) in chasing these lovers? JB (*cf.* GNB) makes it quite deliberate: 'She would not acknowledge, not she, that I was the one...'. But while this would reinforce the blame that God puts on her, the fundamental charge against her is unfaithfulness, to which her lovers' promises have lured her, as it seems from verses 5–7. So the simple translation 'she did not (or, does not) know'[4] seems the truer to the context while still allowing us to comment, 'But she ought to have known!'

In her sin against love there is a further twist of her knife at the end of verse 8, where not only has she ignored the true Giver but has heaped His gifts on His usurper. Once more (we can note in passing) the reader may find himself confronted by a mirror rather than a window, since Israel's sin is also humanity's and everyman's.

The punishment of verses 9–13 is unsparing, yet not unjust; in fact, as the sequel will show in 14ff., far from unfeeling. It is a bitter lesson, but at all costs it must be learnt. In this presentation of it the literal and the metaphorical are intertwined but easily distinguished. There is a bleak prospect of failed harvests and of farms and orchards reverting to the wild (strongly implying in 12b a depopulated land, its inhabitants deported or decimated); and behind it there is the failed promise of the Baals, for whom an infatuated Israel had dolled herself up, flirting with them at the very feasts (11) which were given to cement her union with the Lord.

But the Lord keeps the initiative, not only in judgment but in grace. Suddenly the whole scene lights up.

The constant Lover

2:14 '*Therefore, behold, I will allure her,*
        and bring her into the wilderness,
        and speak tenderly to her.
  15 *And there I will give her her vineyards,*
        and make the Valley of Achor a door of hope.

---

[4] 'Know' is the primary sense of this verb, which turns into 'acknowledge' when followed by a noun or pronoun in some contexts: *e.g.* Je. 3:13; Pr. 3:6.

31

> *And there she shall answer as in the days of her youth,*
> *as at the time when she came out of the land of Egypt.*
> 16 *And in that day, says the Lord, you will call me, "My*
> *husband," and no longer will you call me, "My Baal." [17]For I*
> *will remove the names of the Baals from her mouth, and they*
> *shall be mentioned by name no more.'*

There is a right infatuation (implied in the Hebrew for 'allure her', 14) as well as a disastrous one, for true love need be no less ravishing than false: only less disappointing. The Lord now for His part[5] will exert His charms and speak to the heart[6] of His beloved. This is the positive and creative side of His severity, for 'the wilderness' could mean either of two things for Israel: either her life in ruins or her pilgrim spirit and youthful promise recaptured. Here it offers her the second, by way of the first. The thought of setting out with God is picked up by a later prophet, who sang of that short-lived honeymoon:

> 'I remember the devotion of your youth,
> your love as a bride,
> how you followed me in the wilderness,
> in a land not sown.'[7]

So now, out of disaster and exile the Lord plans to create as fruitful a new era as that which the Exodus had promised to bring in. What has been lost in judgment can be restored in mercy – the ruined vines of verse 12 answered by the vineyards of 15 – and what had spoilt the first victorious progress need not mar the second. That old reproach, the Valley of Achor at the gateway of the promised land (that is, the Valley of Trouble and of Achan's sin; Jos. 7:26), can be not just forgotten but re-named: the Door or Gate of Hope – for when God forgives, He does it handsomely, and in this single line of verse 15 He lays the ghosts of not only Israel's past but, by analogy, the past of any repentant sinner.

---

[5] The 'I' of verse 14 is emphatic.

[6] This is the Heb. idiom for 'speak tenderly'. It is used in contexts of wooing (Gn. 34:3), comforting (Is. 40:2), reassuring (Gn. 50:21), winning round (Jdg. 19:3), showing kindness (Ru. 2:13).

[7] Je. 2:2.

But salvation is not all vineyards and victories, even in the Old Testament, but at its heart the union of God and man. So in verses 15b–17 we are shown the answer God is waiting for, and His concern that it will mean no less than it professes. The confusion at the root of popular religion (which gaily mixes one god with another, and faith with superstition) had been made still worse by the existence of the misleading word Baal. In itself it simply meant 'lord', 'owner' or 'husband', and in early Israel it was sometimes used quite innocently of God, as certain personal names confirm.[8] But in Canaanite religion it stood for the most active god in the pantheon, and for his various other selfs and colleagues, the god of each particular place. It was he, as divine husband, who gave the land its fertility through the rites, sexual and otherwise, performed 'upon every high hill and under every green tree', as Jeremiah 2:20 sweepingly expresses it.

This, then, had been the stain that had spread through Israel wherever the name of Baal painted a pagan image on the name of Yahweh, and brought pagan rites to His pure worship.

So it is a bold and creative stroke by which God, instead of banning sexual imagery from religion, rescues and raises it to portray the ardent love and fidelity which are the essence of His covenant. Having made this clear, He can now go on to show what concord and delight the full flowering of that marriage of God and man will bring.

Perfect bliss

2:18 *'And I will make for you a covenant on that day with the beasts of the field, the birds of the air, and the creeping things of the ground; and I will abolish the bow, the sword, and war from the land; and I will make you lie down in safety.* [19]*And I will betroth you to me for ever; I will betroth you to me in righteousness and in justice, in steadfast love, and in mercy.* [20]*I will betroth you to me in faithfulness; and you shall know the Lord.*

---

[8] Notably Beeliada ('the Lord knows'), a son of David (1 Ch. 14:7), who was also known less controversially as Eliada ('God knows') (2 Sa. 5:16). Jonathan, another loyal Yahwist, called his son Meribbaal (1 Ch. 8:34), but 'Baal' later became regularly changed to 'Bosheth' ('shame'), and Meribbaal has become better known to us as Mephibosheth (whose identity is confirmed by 2 Sa. 9:12).

'That day' (16, 18, 21) points us on, in the Old Testament, to the great day, the Day of the Lord, not simply to a time in the near future. To us that day has dawned already in the First Advent, though it will not reach high noon until the Second.

For all its brevity, this little prophecy entwines together strands which only separately delight us in other more familiar passages. In a few lines we have the picture of nature at peace with man (*cf.* Is. 11:6–9; 65:25), of weapons discarded (*cf.* Ps. 46:9; Is. 9:5; Mi. 4:3) and of God's people at one with Him (*cf.* Je. 31:33f.; Ezk. 36:26f.). It is the last of these that God lingers over, for it is the heart of the matter.

Coming three times in quick succession, the word 'betroth' gives a note of eagerness and warmth to what is promised. It makes it a new beginning, with all the freshness of first love, rather than the weary patching up of differences – and this is appropriate, since the new covenant brings with it new life. Betrothal also goes further than the courtship of verse 14, speaking of a step that was even more decisive in Israelite custom than engagement is with us. It involved handing over the bride-price to the girl's father, whose acceptance of it finalized the matter. David's betrothal to Saul's daughter, at the barbarous price demanded of him, is described in 2 Samuel 3:14 in terms which, in Hebrew, show that the five qualities listed here, ranging from 'righteousness' to 'faithfulness', are thought of as the bride-price which God, the suitor, brings with Him. The metaphor, of course, is imperfect, like the ransom metaphor of Mark 10:45, since there is no 'father of the bride' to receive the gift. But even in literal betrothals such a present could be passed to the bride herself to be her dowry,[9] and certainly she is the beneficiary here.

So the promise overflows with generosity. It is all of grace, and it clothes the New Covenant in wedding garb. It makes three things very plain: the permanence of this union (19a), the intimacy of it (20b), and the fact that it owes everything to God.

But what exactly is this betrothal gift, leaving metaphor aside? Are these the qualities which God will bring to His side of the marriage, or those that He will implant in us, His people?

The answer is surely both. Righteousness, steadfast love and

---

[9] *Cf.* Harper, p. 243, who refers to Gn. 31:15, where Laban has characteristically failed to part with it. Note also the gifts directly given to Rebekah in Gn. 24:53.

the rest are pre-eminently the very stamp and character of God, and it was the lack of them on Israel's side, not on His, that had wrecked the marriage in the first place. So God's gift is that He will not only be to us all these things but will impart them, so that His bride will be no longer in fundamental discord with Him and at odds with herself. It is another way of saying that He will put His law within His people and write it on their hearts (*cf*. Je. 31:33).

Unwrapping, so to speak, the fivefold gift, we find first that in the Bible *righteousness* (Heb. *ṣedeq*) is a warmer and more positive thing than we might have dared to hope. Far from being a cold rectitude preoccupied with keeping its hands clean, true righteousness is active and generous, whether it is seen in God or man (*cf*., *e.g*., Ps. 111:3 with 112:9). 'Its meaning', as Norman Snaith has pointed out,[10] 'has to be found in the nature of God rather than in customs and speculations of man, however noble and splendid these thoughts and ideals may be at their best.' God's righteousness is creative, stepping in to put the very worst things right. It is so often paired with 'salvation' that some modern versions, including RSV, tend to call it 'deliverance' or 'vindication' (*e.g*. Is. 51:5–8; Ps. 98:2); and if this sometimes obscures a large part of its meaning, it captures another important part.

So, in every sense, righteousness is a gift from God; and never more so than when it means His bestowing of acceptance and acquittal on us; or in Paul's expression, 'justification'. Paul found this 'free gift of righteousness' already discernible in the Old Testament (Rom. 4) and now plainly ours to 'receive', by faith in Christ (Rom. 5:17).

The second facet of the betrothal gift is *justice* (Heb. *mišpāṭ*); and this too must have its roots in God and its fruits displayed in us. At bottom it means the rulings of a judge, and while a human judge may be shallow and unfair, God's justice is 'like the depths of the sea' (Ps. 36:6, GNB) – vast, profound and inexhaustible in wisdom, whether He is pronouncing a verdict or revealing His will for us – that proper ordering of life which man, unlike his fellow creatures, regularly disregards.

'Even the stork in the heavens knows her times;

[10] N. H. Snaith, *Mercy and Sacrifice* (SCM Press, 1953), p. 76.

and the turtledove, swallow, and crane
keep the time of their coming;
but my people know not
the ordinance[11] of the Lord.'

The prophets found that religious men are all too happy to combine sacred rites with social wrongs; and if there is one thing that God cannot stand, this is it. Amos puts it most pungently of all (Am. 5:21–24):

'I hate, I despise your feasts, . . . your solemn assemblies . . .
Take away from me the noise of your songs . . .
But let justice roll down like waters,
and righteousness like an ever-flowing stream.'

But it is here in Hosea that justice and righteousness are seen not only as the Lord's demands but as His gifts – certainly to be worked on and cultivated, but gifts none the less.

The third facet, *steadfast love* (Heb. *ḥeseḏ*), might be less cumbersomely called 'devotion' or 'true love'. The older versions called it either 'mercy' or, beautifully, 'lovingkindness'; but an essential part of it is the tacit recognition of an existing bond between the parties it embraces. It implies the love and loyalty which partners in marriage or in covenant owe to one another; so it has a special relevance to what Hosea had been denied by Gomer. God names it in 6:6 as the thing He most desires to see in us. For God's people it sets a standard of mutual kindness and concern among themselves; but it goes further, for in 6:4 it means the love and constancy they owe to God and have so far failed to give Him. As God's bridal gift, then, while it is first and foremost His devoted love towards His partner, we may see it also as the very response He intends to create in her.

The fourth word (Heb. *raḥᵃmîm*) is the warmest of all terms for *mercy*, rather like the word for heartfelt *compassion* found in the parables and personal reactions of Jesus. It has a special link with the name of the child Lo-ruhamah, 'Not-pitied' (1:6), which is formed from the same root. True to His nature, God could not wait to cancel that appalling name. He did so as far

---

[11] Lit. judgment, *i.e.*, *mišpāṭ*, Je. 8:7, the word we are discussing.

back as 2:1; and now, speaking to Israel as His betrothed, He makes assurance doubly sure.

But once again the dowry cannot make the marriage, unless it can also work an inward miracle. The people seen in chapter 4, who 'break all bounds and murder follows murder' (4:2), will treat compassion only as weakness, unless they are given a heart for it themselves. A later prophet, Zechariah, showed just what they had thought of 'justice, steadfast love and mercy', using three of the very terms that come together in our verse (Zc. 7:9ff., Heb.). The 'heart of stone' would never warm towards God or man. So the gentlest of God's gifts is in some ways the most searching.

Finally, *faithfulness* (Heb. *'*emûnâ*). Of all qualities, this is the one most clearly lacking in a partner who has quitted. Other faults may put a marriage under strain; this one is decisive. God, of course, had been faithful all along, under endless provocation; therefore once again the betrothal gift must be not only what He Himself displays but what He will implant and cultivate within His partner.

The second line of verse 20 sums up His gift: *and you shall know the Lord.* This is one of the crowning promises of the New Covenant (Je. 31:34), for true knowledge depends upon true likeness, and to promise the one is to promise the other. The assurance that 'we shall see him as he is' turns out to contain the unimaginable prospect that 'we shall be like him' (1 Jn. 3:2).

Abundant concord

2:21 '*And in that day, says the Lord,*
  I will answer the heavens
  and they shall answer the earth;
 22 *and the earth shall answer the grain, the wine, and the oil,*
  and they shall answer Jezreel;
 23 *and I will sow him for myself in the land.*
  And I will have pity on Not pitied,
  and I will say to Not my people, "You are my people";
  and he shall say, "Thou art my God."'

The picture that we saw in verse 3 of the land under judgment, parched and crying out for relief, may help us to appreciate this sequence of petitions and answers. Tracing it backwards from verse 22b we see certain links in the chain of survival: the people ('Jezreel' – see below) looking to their crops, the crops to the soil, the soil to the sky for rain, the sky to the Lord – and 'in that day', the Day of the Lord,[12] the answer will be an abundant 'Yes!' But in fact the sequence is not traced backwards, but in its proper order beginning with the Lord. And there is more to it than a simple promise of better times to come, for it is an answer also to the labyrinthine world of polytheism, with its one god for corn, one for rain, and so on, which had stolen Israel's heart and had muddled all her thinking. Instead of that tangle of competing powers we see the one Lord from whom all blessings flow, and glimpse the orderly variety of His creation, through which His gifts are mediated not at random but within His perfect will, and not by means of magic but within a created system that makes sense and therefore can be studied and put to use. As H. W. Wolff has pointed out, 'the background of these verses indicates a genuine scientific representation of relationships within nature. . . . In the book of Hosea, it is instructive to note how Israel's liberation from the nature myths of the cult of Baal permitted the free study of nature to flourish (cf. Gen. 1).'[13]

It is worth adding that, however elementary and obvious this model of the natural world may seem, it is elementary in the best sense, for it brings us down to a basic presupposition from which almost every advance in practical knowledge stems: that the world is a single, close-knit composition, intelligible in principle. And it does not make the blunder of exalting that system by denying its fount and origin. So we are not left with a mechanistic world on the one hand, nor with a God who keeps us guessing on the other, but with a world we can explore and a God we can trust and serve responsibly within it.

The climax of this set of promises dispels the last shadow of the oracles of chapter 1. Already this has been anticipated in 1:10 – 2:1; now it is reiterated, and one new thing stands out at once. While the names of Hosea's second and third children ('Not pitied' and 'Not my people') are again set free from their negatives, as in 2:1, the name of the eldest, *Jezreel*, is now

---

[12] See the opening comment on 2:18–20, p. 34.
[13] Wolff, pp. 55f.

reinterpreted. Instead of being a reminder of Jehu and his massacres (see on 1:4), the name will now take its colour from the meaning of its two Hebrew components. The Hebrew *yizr"el* (Jezreel) means 'God will sow', or 'May God sow'; and God now turns this into a promise that His land, long ruined and deserted, will be sown with inhabitants again. He adds, in passing, that this is 'for myself' – for God, like any farmer who takes a pride in what he cultivates, hates to see His beloved land lying useless and His people scattered. His good name is bound up with all this, and for His own sake He will see the situation changed. Ezekiel 36:22ff. takes up the theme, and shows that while this approach may not be flattering it is highly reassuring, for it bases everything on God's honour, nothing on our dubious merits.

There is one other new thing. Where the earlier promise showed God saying affectionate things to Israel, such as 'Sons of the living God' and 'My people' (1:10; 2:1), the last words of our chapter bring back a human reply to Him: '(Thou art) my God.' Like an exchange of marriage vows this mutual affirmation, 'you are mine', was the very heart of the covenant, and still is.

This brings us to the point where we are no longer overhearing a conversation between God and ancient Israel, but finding ourselves involved directly. Twice in the New Testament this 'welcome home' to those who were 'Not pitied' and 'Not my people' is quoted from our two chapters (1:10 – 2:1; 2:23) as God's word now to 'us whom he has called, not from the Jews only but also from the Gentiles'. Paul cites it to demonstrate the unfettered grace of God towards the undeserving (Rom. 9:23– 26); and Peter, to show that in Christ we are not only reconciled but incorporated into 'a chosen race, ... God's own people' (1 Pet. 2:9f.). If this chapter therefore leaves us only contemplating God's way with ten tribes whose kingdom disappeared 2,700 years ago, we have parted company with the New Testament as well as the Old. These things constitute 'the grace', as 1 Peter 1:10 puts it, 'that was to be yours'.

Hosea 3:1–5
'Love . . . as the Lord loves'

Now Hosea rounds off his own story in the first person. He

uses no rhetoric. The humiliating domestic episode is re-counted quietly, factually, and its bigger counterpart and pro-totype explained with equal objectivity. There could be no better prelude than this story to the impassioned chapters that will follow, for it shows us at the outset, as it showed Hosea, the poignant personal demands that are involved in mending any close relationship. This was no arm's-length settling of a legal battle or extracting of apologies. A marriage asks, because it offers, nothing facile or transitory; and God will be offering and asking in the coming chapters only what is from the heart and for all time.

The hard way home (i)

3:1 *And the Lord said to me, 'Go again, love a woman who is beloved of a paramour and is an adulteress; even as the Lord loves the people of Israel, though they turn to other gods and love cakes of raisins.' ² So I bought her for fifteen shekels of silver and a homer and a lethech of barley. ³ And I said to her, 'You must dwell as mine for many days; you shall not play the harlot, or belong to another man; so will I also be to you.'*

It would have been impressive enough had Hosea found that in spite of everything he still loved his truant wife, and had then perceived that God's love must be like that too. But in fact it was the other way about. It was God's love that rekindled Hosea's, when the Lord said 'Go again, love (her)',[1] and gave him the pattern to reproduce.

There was no glossing over the unpleasant truth. The 'again' in God's command faced the fact that old wounds would have to be reopened and that what had happened once might happen yet again. Also the adultery, God reminded him, was still in progress:[2] it had been no isolated lapse but a desertion which added a continuing insult to the injury. The love that was asked

---

[1] There is no ground for rendering this 'Go again and *show* your love . . .' (GNB; my italics). The Hebrew has the simple imperative, 'love', carrying no suggestion that love was already there, merely awaiting an outlet.

[2] Although she is unnamed here, there need be no doubt that the woman in question is Hosea's wife (note the word 'adulteress', implying a married woman. Note too the charge to go to her 'again', and the parallel with Israel, the bride to whom God remains faithful). A variant reading of the expression

of him would be heroic – but that was the point, for it was to be God's love in miniature.

Perhaps this is why Hosea captures, as no other writer does, the tension within God's love for His elect – for He refuses to ease the pain of the relationship either by compromise or by quitting. He loves these people despite their blatant unfaithfulness ('they turn to other gods'), which He cannot for a moment condone, and despite their fatuous and brutish scale of values. Four times this opening verse has spoken in terms of love, each pair of its occurrences placing a noble use of the word in grating proximity to a base one – pure devotion next to gross infatuation. As for the second pair, it ends in utter bathos, with God loving Israel to the uttermost, while Israel gives her heart to (of all things!) *cakes of raisins*. However one may try to soften the jolt of this, by associating these delicacies with religious feasts or rare occasions,[3] the incongruity of it is still outrageous. The bride, it seems, is only here, or anywhere else, for the cakes and ale.

'Screwtape', we may suppose, would have hailed this as an unusually satisfying victory for his department – for a victory it would still have been, even if the bait had had to be the world itself (*cf*. Mk. 8:36). But (to quote that artist in temptation) 'an ever increasing craving for an ever diminishing pleasure is the formula. It is more certain; and it's better *style*. To get the man's soul and give him *nothing* in return – that is what really gladdens our Father's heart'[4] – 'our Father', of course, being Screwtape's term for the father of lies and liars. Few of us, remembering the trivialities we chase, will feel ready to cast the first stone at Israel.

So I bought her ... The reticence is eloquent. In the single word *bought* we learn how far she had fallen, how tightly she was held, and what was the first step Hosea must take to fulfil

---

'beloved of' is possible, *viz*. 'in love with', as found in LXX (which also reads, less plausibly, 'evil', *ra'*, instead of 'paramour' or 'friend', *rēa'*). These alternatives involve only vowel changes, but there is no strong reason for preferring them to the standard text.

[3] David distributed them at the festivities to celebrate the ark's arrival at Jerusalem (2 Sa. 6:19). In a heathen context, Moab mourns the loss of them (Is. 16:7). In the Song of Songs, the cry 'Stay me with flagons' (Song 2:5, AV) is more accurately rendered ' ... with raisin-cakes'.

[4] C. S. Lewis, *The Screwtape Letters* (Bles, 1942), IX.

the command to love her. Our curiosity is not satisfied over the exact reason for the purchase (were these her debts? was she now a slave? perhaps a prostitute working for an owner? or was this the compensation paid to the loving 'boy-friend' of verse 1 – revealing incidentally what his love was worth?). Nor are we told of Hosea's feelings: only how he scraped together the price he had to find.[5] In Scripture, more often than not, love is practical first, emotional only second; and it is always to be known by its fruits. This is not to say that love is 'as cold as charity', for the Old Testament largely uses, as we ourselves do, the same word for love between friends,[6] or between the sexes,[7] as for the love that is the fulfilling of the law. The word takes its colour from its context (as its four occurrences in verse 1 have shown), but it is not complete without both aspects of self-giving: a devoted will and a genuine warmth.

There was realism as well as symbolism in the probationary period of verse 3. Its larger meaning is spelt out in verses 4–6, but within the marriage there were the disloyal habits of years to be broken, and the realities of personal relationship, which had hitherto stopped at the physical level, to be unhurriedly explored together. In the last part of verse 3 the NEB expresses the Hebrew text[8] as well as any: 'and have no intercourse with a man, nor I with you.'

Now follows the meaning of all this for Israel, the truant wife of Yahweh.

The hard way home (ii)

3:4 *For the children of Israel shall dwell many days without king or prince, without sacrifice or pillar, without ephod or teraphim. [5]Afterward the children of Israel shall return and seek the Lord their God, and David their king; and they shall come in fear to the Lord and to his goodness in the latter days.*

---

[5] It seems to have amounted to about 30 shekels, which is the price set on a slave in Ex. 21:32. See Wolff, p. 61, for this calculation. The load of barley was quite large, since a homer = 220 litres = *c.* 6 bushels. If a lethech was half a homer, the total was about 330 litres, or 9 bushels.

[6] *E.g.* 1 Sa. 18:3; 1 Ki. 5:1 (15, Heb.).

[7] *E.g.* Gn. 29:18; Song 1:3, and the verbs throughout this book.

[8] The word 'another' in RSV is borrowed from LXX, whereas the Hebrew would include Hosea himself, who in the final clause is not merely promising to refrain from adultery but speaking of the postponement of marital intercourse.

Remember that a golden half-century was all that Hosea's hearers, for the most part, could recall, even though clouds were now forming in the distance. There was nothing but God's warning through Amos and Hosea to make disaster seem more than a remote possibility.

What is striking about this prophecy is first that it threatens the very pillars of life as Israel knew it, and then that it interprets the withdrawal of all these cherished things – good, bad and indifferent alike – as ultimate gain.

These features of their life were certainly a mixture. At one extreme there was *sacrifice*, a major ordinance of God; at the other, *teraphim* (translated as 'household gods' in Gn. 31:19), objects which violated the second commandment and were vigorously attacked by prophets and reformers from Samuel to Zechariah.[9] Between these extremes, pillar and ephod might be innocent or noxious in different situations,[10] while the existence of *king* and *prince* rather than some foreign governor and his régime had the welcome significance of a country at liberty.

But even the good or neutral things had been corrupted. Their kings and princes had been chosen in self-will ('not through me', says God in 8:4) and in rejection of the house of David; and all their worship was tainted with Baalism. A clean break was needed, deep enough and long enough to make a new beginning possible: a pure return, in all humility, to the Lord Himself; a renewal of the marriage that had seemed beyond repair.

An acid test of their sincerity comes in the words, *and David their king*. In terms of the Israel which Hosea addressed, it meant a climb-down from their pride of independence from the southern tribes – from having their rival king, rival sanctuaries and priests and festivals, and their golden calves (1 Ki. 12:25–33). After the fall of their kingdom in 722 BC there was quite a trickle of such converts back to David's kingdom (see the comments on 1:20 – 2:1, p. 25); but Hosea is looking far into the future to *the latter days*.

We ourselves have seen the dawn of those days ('Children, it is the last hour', 1 Jn. 2:18), and we, as believers, have inherited

[9] See, *e.g.*, 1 Sa. 15:23 (where 'idolatry', RSV, is lit. 'teraphim'); 2 Ki. 23:24; Zc. 10:2.
[10] Contrast the memorial pillars of, *e.g.*, Ex. 24:4 with those of Baal-worship (Dt. 12:3) which probably represented the male deity. Contrast also the ephod as a priestly garment (*e.g.* Ex. 28:4) with its use as an object of worship (Jdg. 8:27).

the name and destiny of Israel (see the final comments on chapter 2). If Israel has taken on a richer meaning, so has *David their king*. Our Lord, in almost His last message to the church, takes up this royal name and proclaims Himself not only David's offspring but also David's origin (Rev. 22:16). So our final verse captures the profound simplicity of the gospel. With the elaborate and humanly corrupted structures of verse 4 swept away, it portrays a people turning, seeking and coming to the Lord and His anointed, with deep penitence,[11] yet – in that they are turning *to his goodness* – with trust in what the New Testament will call His grace.

It may seem too much to see yet another level of fulfilment in this verse. But if (as I take it) Paul predicts in Romans 11:12, 15, 25ff. a great turning of the literal Israel to the Lord at the climax of the gospel era, the present verse may well have added for him its weight of confirmation to the promises he quotes, especially since there are allusions to our chapters not only in Romans 9:25f. but in 11:30f., the verses which round off his prediction.

Even at this early stage in the unfolding of the prophecy we can echo the substance of Paul's ensuing doxology in the remaining verses of Romans 11 – 'O the depth of the riches and wisdom and knowledge of God!' – and more particularly his comment on these riches in Romans 5:20 (AV), 'Where sin abounded, grace did much more abound.' On such a note, of His 'goodness' (3:5), the opening chapters reach their satisfying end.

[11] The expression translated *come in fear to the Lord* could be expressed more literally as 'tremble their way to the Lord'.

Part Two: the parable spelt out
HOW CAN I GIVE YOU UP?
Hosea 4–14

In Part One, with the story and lessons of this extraordinary marriage, the book has already produced in bud the substance of its message, now to be unfolded further in what follows, along with social and political themes not touched on yet. But, more significantly, it has begun to do what no other Old Testament book does quite so vividly: to speak of God and His people not primarily in terms of master and servant, or king and subjects (indispensable as these categories are), but as man and wife, with all that this implies of personal delight and potential hurt.

This approach is far from sentimental. It sharpens guilt immeasurably by making it the betrayal of love; it shows us the true motive of God's persistence, so easily thought to be mere doggedness; and it deepens our understanding of repentance and renewal – for sins against love damage the very roots of a relationship, and are not healed by brisk apologies and hasty resolutions.

So the rest of the book will be packed with detail, whereas the opening chapters have painted the scene with only the broadest brush. It will plead for deep repentance, and it will extend the theme of personal relationships by pursuing that of father and child, as strikingly as the opening oracles explored the man-and-wife analogy.

It will be urgent and rapid, darting from one startling metaphor to another, drawing its pungent comparisons from human occupations, from nature and from Israel's family history. But it will end with an eloquent description of a people who have at last found their way home to God; and its epilogue will urge the reader to take this chequered story well to heart. It is more than a glimpse into history: it reveals the ways of God and the paths of life and death.

Hosea 4:1–19
A people without understanding

Any complacency which the happy ending of the first three chapters may have induced in the reader (if he has begun to picture God as the ever-accommodating husband) is now abruptly shattered. We are suddenly in a court of law, and God is prosecuting.[1] He has no lack of charges to bring.

All the sins in the book

4:1 *Hear the word of the Lord, O people of Israel;*
for the Lord has a controversy with the
inhabitants of the land.
There is no faithfulness or kindness,
and no knowledge of God in the land;
2 *There is swearing, lying, killing, stealing*
and committing adultery;
they break all bounds and murder follows murder.
3 *Therefore the land mourns,*
and all who dwell in it languish,
and also the beasts of the field,
and the birds of the air;
and even the fish of the sea are taken away.

The indictment is all the more telling in that it starts with what God pre-eminently looks for. He is weighing Israel in the balance against *faithfulness*, *kindness* and the *knowledge of God*, only to find her wanting at every point: utterly light on all the things that matter. These three expressions lead us in from the outskirts of goodness to its heart and centre, and at each point God finds in His people this fatal lack. 'Faithfulness' (Heb. *'emet̠*) is common honesty or reliability, the first

---

[1] 'A controversy' (1) is better translated 'a charge' (NEB, NIV) or 'an accusation' (GNB).

ingredient that we require for any dealings, however distant or impersonal, with our fellow men. 'Kindness' (Heb. *ḥeseḏ*, an important word with Hosea[2]) throws another weight into the scales, for it is the love and loyalty expected of partners in covenant – and this partnership was meant to embrace both the Lord and all one's fellow Israelites. What should have been a home and family had turned into a den of lust and violence.

As for the third and chief requirement, the 'knowledge of God', any claim to it was already denied by the absence of the first two qualities. But note how high this last demand is pitched: not for a bare minimum of godliness, a decent fear of the Lord, fundamental though this is, but for a developed and developing relationship – for God is known as He is walked with and as His interests are shared and served. ('Your father … judged the cause of the poor and needy; then it was well. *Is not this to know me?* says the Lord.'[3]) We shall meet this high demand of fellowship again in the famous summary of what God most desires of man ('steadfast love and not sacrifice, the knowledge of God, rather than burnt offerings', 6:6), and shall be reminded in 13:4–5 of the grace that makes it possible: 'You (shall) know no God but me … *It was I who knew you* in the wilderness, in the land of drought.' In this book we are never far away from the warmly personal, marital and father-child relationships as we explore God's expectations of us and His attitudes towards us.

Now follows in verse 2 the ugly catalogue of sins, a dark shadow of the Ten Commandments on their manward side. Each of these evils meets us here full-blown, for it is a time of decadence and they have flourished virtually unchecked.

Scripture in general has two things to say about such rampant wickedness. On the one hand it may question the boundaries we draw between serious and light offences, and between actions and attitudes, seeing for example (to go through this list) an inconsiderate word as little better than a curse (Pr. 27:14), insincerity as nothing but a lie (Jn. 8:55), hatred as

---

[2] It is the word usually translated 'lovingkindness' in AV, RV, but in more recent versions the emphasis is on the element of constancy. *E.g.*, RSV chiefly translates it as 'steadfast love' (*cf.* 2:19; 6:6; 10:12), though here it has 'kindness', and at 6:4 and 12:6, 'love'.

[3] Je. 22:15f.

murder (1 Jn. 3:15), meanness as theft (Mal. 3:8ff.), and lustful imaginings as mental adultery (Mt. 5:28). From its embryonic to its adult form, so to speak, a sin may change its names and its ability to hurt, but not its nature. That is one emphasis. The other is the one implicit here: that there is such a thing as monstrous and scarlet sin; that it is the business of teachers and rulers to restrain it (as the rest of the chapter and of the book will emphasize); and that the 'rank growth of wickedness' – to borrow a phrase from James 1:21 – can reach a point where it is beyond all remedy.[4] In Hosea that point is very near, and judgment must fall; but the punishment may yet produce a change of heart – a hope that runs through the book from the early chapters on the healing of the marriage to the final prospect of a blissful reunion in chapter 14.

Meanwhile to us, with our modern interest in ecology, born of our new ability to make a desert of the world, the ensuing picture of a poisoned environment in verse 3 is all too familiar. But there is no reason to take it as describing Hosea's contemporary scene (as do RSV and JB), for the tenses are those that normally indicate the future. It is a preview of God's judgment on corporate sin, which 'when it is full-grown brings forth death' on a wider scale than had once seemed possible. The Bible stresses sometimes the direct action of God in such a judgment, but sometimes too the reaction of His natural world to man's unnatural handling of it. It is put vividly in Leviticus 18, where a catalogue of perversions culminates in a warning, 'lest the land vomit you out, when you defile it, as it vomited out the nation that was before you' (Lv. 18:28). If this language leaves out many links in the chain of causation, it is not hard to supply a few of them once one recognizes violence, lust and perversion as symptoms of the state of mind which will stop at no restraints and will sacrifice a whole future to the cravings of the moment. Hosea speaks here even more immediately to us, who are approaching the terminal stage of this infection, than to his own generation.

The guiltiest party

4:4 *Yet let no one contend,*

---

[4] See, *e.g.*, Je. 7:16; Rev. 18.

> *and let none accuse,*
> *for with you is my contention, O priest.*
> 5 *You shall stumble by day,*
> *the prophet also shall stumble with you by night;*
> *and I will destroy your mother.*
> 6 *My people are destroyed for lack of knowledge;*
> *because you have rejected knowledge,*
> *I reject you from being a priest to me.*
> *And since you have forgotten the law of your God,*
> *I also will forget your children.*

Whatever we may make of verse 4 (which is not as simple as it may look in our versions[5]), verse 6 removes all doubt that God's chief target is – in modern terms – the clergy. We can use that rough equivalent because it is the priests in their neglected capacity as teachers, not as sacrificers, who are now under fire. The prophets are no better, but here they are not the main concern.

What is even more striking than the poor showing of these men is the glory of the task entrusted to them: no less than to be the nation's spiritual educators. Unlike most religions, where priests were the close guardians of the cultic mysteries while the people's part was more or less mechanical, the faith of the Old Testament was a revelation addressed to every mind and conscience, 'making wise the simple'. Already in this chapter we have come across this theme, noting its profundity (see p. 47). Now we see it as not only profound but crucial: a matter of life and death. So a spiritually sightless priest is a mortal danger to himself and a disaster to others – for Hosea spells out in detail what Christ would one day sum up unforgettably in His saying on the blind who lead the blind (Mt. 15:14). The metaphor of stumbling in verse 5 leads on inexorably to harsher terms: 'destroyed', 'rejected' and 'forgotten'; words which embrace the whole familiar world of these defaulters – their motherland, their priesthood, their posterity.

There is wrath as well as logic here, for the stumbling itself was no accident. All is traced to the emphatic 'you' and to an act of

---

[5] RSV in 4b, as above (with which most of the newer versions broadly concur) fits the context well, but assumes that the Massoretic Text has suffered slightly in transmission. The latter reads, as in AV, RV, NIV, 'for thy people are as they that strive with a priest'.

will, as the Hebrew of verse 6 expresses it: 'because *you* have rejected knowledge...'. And all is clinched in turn by God's no less emphatic '*I also*', which brings the Hebrew sentence to a close.

Like people, like priest

4:7   *The more they increased,*
      the more they sinned against me;
     I will change their glory into shame.
  8   *They feed on the sin of my people;*
      they are greedy for their iniquity.
  9   *And it shall be like people, like priest;*
      I will punish them for their ways,
     and requite them for their deeds.
 10 *They shall eat, but not be satisfied;*
      they shall play the harlot, but not multiply;
    because they have forsaken the Lord
    to cherish harlotry.

While it may look at first sight as if the Lord is speaking of the nation, growing in sin as it grows in size, the 'they' of verse 8 means certainly the priests; therefore these men are surely the subject of verse 7 as well. 'The more priests there are,' as NEB puts it, 'the more they sin against me.' And we can recognize the picture. A protected and exclusive group will easily grow arrogant, and then cynical and shameless. Added to this there was the tempting fact that the sin-offerings, which were prime lambs or kids, were priestly perquisites: 'the priest who offers it for sin shall eat it' (Lv. 6:26).

So the charge of verse 8, 'They feed on the sin of my people', may be quite literal. To a degenerate set of priests, the more sin the better: there would be all the more fresh meat. The fact that the sin-offering was 'a thing most holy', 'given to you' (as Moses reminded Aaron in Lv. 10:17) 'that you may bear the iniquity of the congregation, to make atonement for them', would mean nothing to them. On the other hand, since in times of moral decadence consciences grow hard, and sacrifices scarce, the meaning may be metaphorical: simply that the priests love and relish the prevailing wickedness.[6]

[6] As a point of detail, not affecting the above alternatives, the Heb. words

So comes the blunt prediction, *'like people, like priest'* – a saying which, taken on its own, might either brand the priests as, so to speak, clerical chameleons, for ever matching their colour to their social context (a phenomenon by no means obsolete), or else, as the Hebrew idiom would equally allow, it might imply the converse: that the people would be sinking to the level of their priests.[7] But in fact it is a saying about judgment: a warning that there will be no exemptions. No privilege will shelter this supposed élite. There is a strikingly similar prophecy in Isaiah 24:1–3, speaking of the end time, where the same Hebrew phrase, 'like people, like priest', heads a list ('as with the slave, so with his master', and so on) which demonstrates the equal exposure of us all to the day of God.

The terms of the coming judgment, as initially announced in verse 10, are distinctly appropriate. Food and sex have been these priests' obsession: food and sex will fail them, the one by shortage, the other by sterility – for it is a theme of Scripture and a fact of life that things material are precarious, and things merely sensual frustrating. Our Lord captured both these limitations in a single aphorism: 'Every one who drinks of this water will thirst again' (Jn. 4:13). Of course, to 'play the harlot' is a metaphor here for flirting with false gods; but it had a special aptness in view of the ritual fornication that was part of the attraction of these rivals, as verse 14b reminds us.

So, in what follows, the sins of the flesh and of the spirit intermingle. 'The fear of the Lord is clean'; but even the noblest of other religions and philosophies can do little to cleanse the thoughts of men; and Canaanite religion perhaps least of all.

Creeping corruption

4:11 *Wine and new wine*
take away the understanding.

---

rendered here 'they are greedy for' (8) are generally translated elsewhere by some such expression as 'to set one's heart on' something. *Cf.* Dt. 24:15; Pr. 19:18. There is an instructive pair of occurrences in Pss. 24:4 and 25:1 (RSV 'lift up his/my soul').

[7] The Heb. expression views the likeness as so complete that the parties compared can appear in either order. In, *e.g.*, Gn. 18:25 the order is the opposite to the one we would employ ('as the righteous, so the wicked'), but elsewhere it may coincide with our use: *e.g.* Nu. 15:15, 'as you are, so shall the sojourner be'.

12 *My people inquire of a thing of wood,*
   and their staff gives them oracles,
For a spirit of harlotry has led them astray,
   and they have left their God to play the harlot.
13 *They sacrifice on the tops of the mountains,*
   and make offerings upon the hills,
under oak, poplar, and terebinth,
   because their shade is good.

   Therefore your daughters play the harlot,
      and your brides commit adultery.
14 *I will not punish your daughters when they play the harlot,*
   nor your brides when they commit adultery;
for the men themselves go aside with harlots,
   and sacrifice with cult prostitutes,
and a people without understanding shall come to ruin.

In the Hebrew Bible the first word of this passage is 'harlotry', coming before 'wine and new wine' at the start of verse 11;[8] and the theme of unchastity, both figurative and literal, will dominate the paragraph. This opening thrust has the sound of a proverb, and Hosea will clinch the message with another at the end of verse 14. Both of these sayings chime in with the charge against the priests that they had left their people at the mercy of any folly that took their fancy – 'destroyed' (as verse 6 has put it) 'for lack of knowledge'.

In itself, the proverb about whoredom and wine makes the point that what unbridled drinking does to blur the mind, unbridled sex will also do in its more subtle way. This is a remark well suited to a pleasure-loving Israel; but Hosea makes the further point that spiritual wantonness, the deserting of God for idols, is equally bemusing. The very fact that a people once enlightened by the living God could turn to bits of wood for guidance – praying to a wooden idol and, for divination,

---

[8] It is transposed to the end of verse 10 in the layout of *BH* and *BHS* and of most modern versions, to provide an object to 'cherish' at the end of that verse. It may have originally come twice, ending verse 10 and opening 11, and have dropped out once in the copying (such 'haplography' is a common slip of the pen); or else verse 10 should perhaps be translated, with RV, '... left off to take heed to the Lord'. The prominence of harlotry in 11–14 supports the inclusion of the word here, in agreement with the Massoretic punctuation.

studying the way a stick thrown up at random might fall and point (*cf.* Ezk. 21:21) – told its tale of spiritually-clouded minds. Such things were for 'the heathen in his blindness'. 'These nations', Moses had said of the Canaanites, 'give heed to soothsayers and to diviners; but as for you, the Lord your God has not allowed you so to do. The Lord your God will raise up for you a prophet like me from among you, from your brethren – him you shall heed' (Dt. 18:14–15). As for idols, the heathen themselves should have known better than to worship them, but their minds were darkened and in bondage (Is. 44:18–20).

Whatever excuse there might be for these other nations, for Israel there was none. Their infatuation was deliberate, a surrender to 'a spirit of harlotry' that had all the excitement of an elopement or an orgy. This, they felt, was freedom! Instead of high demands on mind and will there were the myths and magic of the corn god. Instead of the remoteness of the temple, so unfairly situated in the rival capital, Jerusalem, there was the appeal of hilltop sanctuaries to local pride and superstition, and the attractiveness of tree-shrines 'because' (as God observes with fine scorn) 'their shade is good'! Hosea's runaway wife had felt the lure of just such trivialities in her escape from home and husband.

But the language of adultery and prostitution was not all metaphor. This society had gone as sex-mad as our own, with promiscuous adolescents and with marriages violated from the start. Hosea takes an unexpected line on this, for instead of castigating the juvenile prostitutes ('your daughters') and the roving brides, he asks who has set them this example. The answer is the men – the very fathers and husbands who felt themselves betrayed.

Verse 14 is in fact a landmark in moral history by its refusal to treat a man's sexual sins more leniently than a woman's. That double standard had been brutally taken for granted, long before, by Jacob's fourth son Judah, who thought nothing of visiting a prostitute but reacted to his daughter-in-law's apparent unchastity with 'Bring her out, and let her be burned' (Gn. 38:24).

The whole paragraph in fact insists on joining together what we might wish to treat as separate issues. It looked first at self-indulgent, mindless religion; found it guilty of producing spiritual adultery ('they have left their God to play the harlot'); saw this in turn as the direct cause of moral breakdown (note the 'Therefore' of verse 13c); brought to light men's heavy share in women's guilt; and in the same breath swept aside the accepted difference between going with harlots and going with cult-prostitutes. This last point throws a lurid light on Canaanite religion, which owed much of its appeal to the belief that one's crops could be magically made fertile through a sacrifice and sex act at the sanctuary. The fact that our terms, 'cult prostitutes', 'temple prostitutes' and the like, translate a single word meaning literally 'holy women', shows the unbridgeable gulf between the values of the two religions. Biblical and pagan holiness do not inhabit the same world.

One might add that the modern paganism which sees profundity in the 'dark gods', and more sublimity in a *grande passion* than in a single steadfast love, is as fatal a parody of the truth as was Baalism in its time. But today the concept in dispute is not holiness, which only one side talks about, but love.

The passage is capped in 14c by a tersely devastating saying – just four words in the Hebrew – which could well be coupled with the verse which introduced the paragraph, thus (freely):

> (11) Wenching and wining addle the mind
> (14c) And the folk that won't think won't survive.

No political initiatives, no social engineering, could save a people in this state of mindless apostasy. Nothing but repentance.

Keep your distance!

4:15 *Though you play the harlot, O Israel,*
> *let not Judah become guilty.*
> *Enter not into Gilgal,*
>> *nor go up to Beth-aven,*
>> *and swear not, 'As the Lord lives.'*
16 *Like a stubborn heifer,*
> *Israel is stubborn;*
> *can the Lord now feed them*
>> *like a lamb in a broad pasture?*

17 *Ephraim is joined to idols,*
> *let him alone.*

18 *A band of drunkards, they give themselves to harlotry;*
   they love shame more than their glory.
19 *A wind has wrapped them in its wings,*
   and they shall be ashamed because of their altars.

Irony, bitter irony, is surely the clue to this sudden shout of warning to the neighbouring Judah. It is unimaginative to ask what such a change of audience is doing here,[9] or whether it is Israel or Judah who is being warned away from the places and practices of verse 15. As Mays points out, 'Whether Judeans were inclined to visit Gilgal and Bethel is beside the point. The exhortation to Judah not to visit Israel's favourite shrines is ... meant for the ears of those who did worship in them.' It was a startling, infuriating thing for Israelites to hear – far more effective than a straight onslaught.

Hosea is in fact taking a leaf out of Amos's book. Amos, a lover of surprise, had ironically invited his readers to both these famous shrines to deepen their – guilt! 'Come to Bethel, and transgress...' (Am. 4:4). Join our pilgrimage and earn a black mark! Hosea's variation on the theme gets under the skin at two fresh points. It makes a wounding comparison, presenting Israel as no fit company for her smaller sister; and it invents a nickname for the royal shrine: no longer Bethel, 'house of God', but Beth-aven, 'house of evil' – for God cannot own such a place, or have His name bandied about by those who think of Him as Baal. You cannot keep the third commandment, against taking His name in vain, while you blithely flout the first two.

If we want a modern equivalent, it could well be the religious pluralism expressed in the studied neutrality of certain courses on world religions, or of any multi-faith service. 'Come to St. X's and blaspheme', a modern Amos might say. And a modern Hosea, 'Don't darken its doors! You must choose between that and God.'

What follows in the rest of this short passage brings to mind

[9] A common suggestion is that a later editor has sought to widen the relevance of the book by inserting this and other references to the sister kingdom of Judah. This is easy to assert, but the frequency of such passages (1:1, 7, 11; 4:15; 5:5, 10, 12–14; 6:4, 11; 8:14; 10:11; 11:12; 12:2), the breadth of vision of other prophets (*e.g.*, Amos of Judah prophesied to Israel), and the similar temptations that beset both kingdoms, tell against the assumption that Hosea would have had no thoughts for the southerners.

our Lord's lament, 'How often would I ..., and you would not!' (Mt. 23:37). The question,[10] 'Can' (or more accurately, 'Will') 'the Lord ...?' (16b) confronts us with the obstinate realities of the situation, and there will be still more searching questions later, notably in 6:4 and in God's anguished soliloquy of chapter 11. For the moment, in face of such stubbornness, nothing will win a right response. The prodigal must be left to his boon companions (this is the force of RSV's word 'joined', 17) and to his revels and their aftermath. Not till then (and here not till the last line of the chapter) is there any prospect of his coming to himself.

Hosea 5:1–14
The prospect darkens

For several chapters now the picture will be building up by fragments, coming at the subject from all kinds of angles. By its very disjointedness the style suits the chaotic situation it addresses. Here and there in this chapter some belated stirrings of national alarm will be detected; but what action it will lead to is quite another matter. How deep or shallow is the change of mood will be the question particularly faced in chapter 6. Meanwhile God's exposure of His people and of what must happen to them continues in a hail of strong and lively metaphors.

A nation to avoid

5:1 *Hear this, O priests!*
Give heed, O house of Israel!
Hearken, O house of the king!
For the judgment pertains to you;
for you have been a snare at Mizpah,
and a net spread upon Tabor.
2 *And they have made deep the pit of Shittim;*
but I will chastise all of them.

[10] Literally it has the form of a statement, but spoken with an irony that dismisses it, as the context demands. *Cf.*, *e.g.*, Gn. 3:1, 'So God has actually said ...!'; or Gn. 18:12, 'Sarah laughed to herself, saying, "After I have grown old ... I shall have pleasure!"' – interpreted in the next verse as meaning, 'Shall I indeed ...?'

So far, the brunt of the attack has been on the priests (4:4ff.). Now God rounds on those who have so willingly been led by them. The royal court will have its special reprimand in chapter 7:1–7, but for the present all three estates of the realm are equally under fire.[1]

God sees them as a menace – this people called to be a blessing to the world! The label once fastened on the Canaanites, and also proverbially on prostitutes, comparing them to snares and traps, must now be pinned upon the Chosen People. The place-names of verse 1 were famous in their history: Mizpah was associated perhaps with Jacob, perhaps with Jephthah, Samuel and Saul (for there were several places bearing this name, 'the watch tower'), and Tabor with the great victory of Deborah and Barak. Now they were infamous. To get caught up with what was done there was to wander into a trap, like some hapless bird or beast.

Hosea's audience would need no telling why he was attacking these places; and even we, without their local knowledge, have the clue we need in 4:13. If many an ordinary hilltop had its Baal shrine, wooing dozens of frequenters away from the true faith, the shrines on high places as famous as Mizpah and Mount Tabor would seduce their hundreds.[2]

A modern prophet would scandalize even the faithful if he started naming the equivalents of apostate Mizpah and Tabor. Among the theological faculties where would he begin? Where would he end? Which of them poses no threat to the faith of its initiates? And among the vocational colleges and seminaries, the societies, movements and churches? As the reader will observe, the present author lacks the courage of Hosea; but, more to the point, he lacks Hosea's infallibility! The applica-

---

[1] Possibly, however, since 'judgment' can mean 'justice', the fourth line of verse 1 intensifies the guilt of those in authority by saying that justice is their (neglected) responsibility (cf. JB). Yet such a meaning, if intended, could have been expressed more plainly.

[2] 'The pit of Shittim' (RSV; cf. GNB) slightly emends a difficult Heb. text. It provides a third place-name and variety of trap, but remains a conjecture. The existing text appears to mean 'and devious men (or apostates) have deepened slaughter' (cf. NIV). 'Deepened' is interpreted by JB as 'are entrenched in', and by NEB as 'have shown base (ingratitude)'. G. R. Driver (JTS 34 (1933), p. 40) argues for the meaning 'they deepened the corruption (i.e., fornication) of Shittim' – a reference to the notorious incident of Nu. 25:1ff.

tion of the prophet's words is better done by self-examination; but it should indeed be done.

No short way home

5:3 *I know Ephraim,*
and Israel is not hid from me;
For now, O Ephraim, you have played the harlot,
Israel is defiled.
4 *Their deeds do not permit them*
to return to their God.
For the spirit of harlotry is within them,
and they know not the Lord.

5 *The pride of Israel testifies to his face;*
Ephraim shall stumble in his guilt;
Judah also shall stumble with them.
6 *With their flocks and herds they shall go*
to seek the Lord,
but they will not find him;
he has withdrawn from them.
7 *They have dealt faithlessly with the Lord;*
for they have borne alien children.
Now the new moon shall devour them with their fields.

We can be grateful to the NEB for the affectionate tone it gives to the opening words, translating them as

'I have cared for Ephraim
and I have not neglected Israel;
but now . . .'

– for even though this may press the declaration 'I *know* Ephraim' rather far, it rightly draws attention to Ephraim's unresponsiveness (4b, 'they know not'/'care nothing for'), and it makes the valid point that God's knowing is never perfunctory or cold. To Hosea, of all the prophets, this was crucial; and elsewhere in the Old Testament the deep thrust of God's knowledge, however painful it may initially be, is seen as something to be welcomed, for it means that He knows the worst, and yet persists with us. 'I have seen his ways, but I will heal him' (Is. 57:18).

But there is no pretence here that reconciliation can be easy, or penitence a mere gesture of apology. The whole book is, from one angle, a study of what it means to turn back to God. So in this passage the nation is confronted with two unconsidered facts: the stranglehold of its own habits, and the hiddenness of God for worshippers who are insincere.

The first of these is swiftly demonstrated, point after point, in verses 4 and 5. To say that 'their deeds do not permit them to return' may well have a double meaning: not only that the sinner is the prisoner of his habits, but that his actions, persisted in, will unsay his pious words. The second half of the verse delves deeper, beneath the habits to the fickle spirit, and beneath the fickleness itself to the fundamental lack: 'they know not the Lord'. This is the hiatus at the heart of all nominal religion. But verse 5 points out another obstacle to a reunion. Sin not only alienates: it saddles one with guilt – and guilt is written all over this nation, not by the shamefaced looks that normally betray it, but by the very brazenness that would deny it.

So they must learn that God is not the prisoner of His sacraments. Verse 6 sees them going through the due procedures of religion, sparing no expense to gain access to God; but there is nobody at home. It is a spectacle that meets us in all the prophets of the time; for this was a religious age, and if there is one thing more odious to God than plain iniquity it is what Isaiah 1:13 calls 'iniquity and solemn assembly' – surpliced sin, aggravated in this case by the fertility rites which produced a crop of bastards ('alien children') in both senses of the word, literal and spiritual. All this may explain the cryptic mention of the disastrous 'new moon'[3] in verse 7, for (as Isaiah went on to say) 'Your new moons and your appointed feasts my soul hates'. The very festivals that were relied on to placate God would be the sharpest provocation of Him.

Yet His anger is that of love, not hate. His relentless harrying of them is designed to bring them home, as passage after passage will make plain.

[3] This could mean 'a month will (suffice to) devour them' (cf. AV). Dividing the words differently and revocalizing them, NEB reads 'an innovator', which it interprets as 'an invader'. Other suggestions ('destroyer', 'locust', etc.) assume a miscopying of consonants (cf. LXX, but not the other Greek versions). The standard text, however, as in RV, RSV, is intelligible and pungent.

Deep trouble

5:8 *Blow the horn in Gibeah,*
    the trumpet in Ramah.
  Sound the alarm at Beth-aven;
    tremble, O Benjamin!
  9 *Ephraim shall become a desolation*
    in the day of punishment;
  among the tribes of Israel
    I declare what is sure.
10 *The princes of Judah have become*
    like those who remove the landmark;
  upon them I will pour out
    my wrath like water.
11 *Ephraim is oppressed, crushed in judgment,*
    because he was determined to go after vanity.
12 *Therefore I am like a moth to Ephraim,*
    and like dry rot to the house of Judah.

13 *When Ephraim saw his sickness,*
    and Judah his wound,
  then Ephraim went to Assyria,
    and sent to the great king.
  But he is not able to cure you
    or heal your wound.
14 *For I will be like a lion to Ephraim,*
    and like a young lion to the house of Judah.
  I, even I, will rend and go away,
    I will carry off, and none shall rescue.

The first part of the chapter brought us up short with its double rebuff to Israel. God was withdrawing, we were told (6), and judgment was imminent (7). Now we pick up the second of these threads, leaving the threat of withdrawal to reappear in the next section, where it will introduce one of the book's most notable chapters.

For the present, then, the theme is national disaster. It was no empty threat: the northern kingdom (called both 'Israel' and 'Ephraim' in these chapters) was wiped out in 722 BC, and the southern kingdom, Judah and Benjamin, was brought to its knees in 701, surviving by a hair's breadth, only to collapse little more than a century later.

The place-names that open this oracle (8) straddle the border of the two kingdoms – a warning that the invader would penetrate Israel right to its southernmost extremity, to the alarm of the Benjaminite Gibeah and Ramah, which lay only just beyond that boundary, even as the doomed Beth-aven (*i.e.*, Bethel, see on 4:15) lay just within it.

They might well tremble. If Israel was a den of vice, Judah was a den of thieves – for the habit of land-grabbing in verse 10[4] is witnessed by the contemporary Micah and Isaiah:

> They covet fields, and seize them;
> and houses, and take them away;
> they oppress a man and his house,
> a man and his inheritance (Mi. 2:2).

> Shame on you! you who add house to house
> and join field to field,
> until not an acre remains,
> and you are left to dwell alone in the land
> (Is. 5:8, NEB).

The opening alarm-calls presage war; but the human invader is so clearly a mere tool of judgment that he goes unmentioned here. God's anger and God's action are everything, and the different roles in which He now appears are startling and instructive. When He likens Himself to a panther (14, NEB) or a lion, it is no stylized picture but a lifelike predator, grimly purposeful and dangerous. But verse 12 presents a quite novel impression of God in action, 'like a moth[5] ... and like dry rot' (or caries?) – for the silent process of decay is His, no less than the march of armies. Both can be well accounted for in natural terms when a nation goes soft, but both are God's potential scourges, as appropriate as they are deadly. Of the

---

[4] This may, however, be an analogy for the removal of moral landmarks. The expression, 'like those ...', may indicate either this analogy or a comparison of these expropriating creditors and officials with the criminals who surreptitiously moved boundary stones, attracting the curse of Dt. 27:17.

[5] Or possibly 'like putrefaction' (K-B), a conjecture by G. R. Driver from an Arabic root. Although this is precarious it gains some probability from verse 13's allusion to an unhealed wound.

two threats to a people, aggression and corruption, the second is the more ominous, and in these chapters its signs are everywhere. Aggression, for all its terrors, can unite and purge, but corruption only divides and demoralizes.

But when this nation does wake up to its predicament, according to this chapter its reaction is typically shallow. To save its skin – never mind its soul! – it flies straight to Assyria,[6] asking itself no questions about the kind of patron it is getting, still less about the kind of cure it really needs.

What makes the deal look even less promising is the probability that Hosea is speaking of the desperate payment scraped together for Assyria by Israel's King Menahem. This was meant not only to buy off an invasion already begun, but to get external backing for Menahem's precarious kingship – for he was a usurper who had waded through particularly vile slaughter to the throne. His story, which included the butchery of a whole town's pregnant women, is summarized in 2 Kings 15:16–22.

To us, who know the eventual outcome, there is heavy irony in this diplomatic stroke. Menahem's régime was duly propped up, but within twenty years Assyria proved to be the very nation marked out as Israel's executioner.

With some premonition of this, Israel would soon start flitting from one great power to another, playing off Egypt against Assyria, and Assyria against Egypt. The later chapters will have many remarks about it. But first there is a glimmer of light, for which our present chapter's final verse will set the scene.

Hosea 5:15 – 7:2
Let us press on to know the Lord

Here we reach a high point among the foot-hills of the prophecy, from which we catch a tantalizing glimpse of the distant summit, the final chapter. Even though we plunge

[6]'The great king' (13) makes an appropriate parallel to 'Assyria', whose kings used such a title. The Heb. text allows this if its consonants are redivided and revocalized; and this seems a reasonable reconstruction. As it stands, however, it reads 'king Jareb' (AV, RV), *i.e.*, 'a king who finds fault' (*cf.* RSV mg.), or 'King Pick-Quarrel' (G. A. Smith) – a fitting enough label for Tiglath-pileser III and his successors.

almost immediately into as dark a valley as any that we encounter, we have first had an unforgettable if only momentary view of a goal worth reaching at any cost.

The reunion God longs for

5:15 *I will return again to my place,*
until they acknowledge their guilt and seek my face,
and in their distress they seek me, saying,
6:1 *'Come, let us return to the Lord;*
for he has torn, that he may heal us;
he has stricken and he will bind us up.
2 *After two days he will revive us;*
on the third day he will raise us up,
that we may live before him.
3 *Let us know, let us press on to know the Lord;*
his going forth is sure as the dawn;
he will come to us as the showers,
as the spring rains that water the earth.'

4 *What shall I do with you, O Ephraim?*
What shall I do with you, O Judah?
Your love is like a morning cloud,
like the dew that goes early away.
5 *Therefore I have hewn them by the prophets,*
I have slain them by the words of my mouth,
and my judgment goes forth as the light.
6 *For I desire steadfast love and not sacrifice,*
the knowledge of God, rather than burnt offerings.

There was a warning earlier on (5:6) that Israel would one day seek the Lord but find no trace of Him:

... they will not find him;
he has withdrawn from them.

Now we look at both sides of this. First the withdrawal. From one angle, this is only what the fickle wife deserves, so long as she plays fast and loose with her true partner; and God has already spoken in terms of such deserving. Yet even the outburst of chapter 2, which threatened famine and disgrace as her due punishment (2:13, summing up a catalogue of ordeals), had melted into the language of appeal and courtship:

> 'Therefore, behold, I will allure her,
>   and bring her into the wilderness,
>   and speak tenderly to her'   (2:14).

Throughout the book this is the longed-for outcome of His judgments. Whatever else might be their character, they are pre-eminently a lover's short-lived coolness to reawaken love.

But what are we to make of Israel's response?

As God describes it (5:15) and quotes it (6:1–3), it is a model of repentance, entreaty and trust. Yet He seems to greet it with profound misgiving in verses 4ff.

There are at least two ways of taking this. One is that God is first portraying in 5:15 – 6:3 the deep conversion that He is working for and will at last evoke – that total change of heart which will irradiate the closing chapter of the book. Then in verses 4ff. He turns to the sad spectacle of Israel as she is at present, incapable of any such response. On this view (or on the view that verses 1–3 are Hosea's own plea to Israel – see below, p. 65) no fault can be found with the sentiments of these verses. In themselves they are a perfect expression of humility, faith and serious intent. The trouble is that Israel is at present in no state to speak or even think along such lines. Religion, for her, is not *knowing* God, still less 'pressing on to know him'. It is merely placating Him with sacrifice, as verse 6 implies.

A more common view[1] is that the fine words of verses 1–3 are Israel's own, but facile and presumptuous, as if to say with Catherine the Great, *'Le bon Dieu pardonnera; c'est son métier'* – 'The good Lord will pardon; that's his trade' – making light of both the desperate state of the nation ('after two days he will revive us') and the high demands of pressing on to know the Lord. Against this one might point out that this speech is introduced in 5:15 as something spoken out of deep distress, and that the second word for 'seek' in that verse is especially urgent ('seek earnestly': *cf.* NEB, NIV). Yet a similar passage in the Psalms reveals how false such earnestness can be:

---

[1] *Cf.* the headings in JB, GNB, and the light-hearted tone adopted in the latter's rendering of 6:1–3.

When he slew them, they sought for him;
    they repented and sought God earnestly (*sic*).
. . . But they flattered him with their mouths;
    they lied to him with their tongues.
Their heart was not steadfast toward him
                    (Ps. 78:34, 36–37).

Either view, then, is possible, and either way it emerges that Israel has no conception of the faithful love that God is looking for. But to me it is the former view that carries conviction, if only because the divine protest in verse 6 makes no contact – except by way of agreement! – with anything in verses 1–3. It also allows us to read these verses as the eloquent and rich example of a serious approach to God which they appear to be. They are restored to us as words not only for study but for actual use.

To look at the passage, then, more closely, it is significant that the word '*saying*', at the end of 5:15 (RSV; *cf.* GNB), is no part of the Hebrew text, but is borrowed from the Septuagint. Without it, we are free to read 6:1–3 either as the expected words of Israel or as Hosea's own call to his compatriots: an inspired appeal for which, however, Israel is not yet remotely ready (as verses 4ff. make clear), although one day she will be (as chapter 14 foresees).

There are several further points to notice in this great passage (as I regard it), above and beyond those that lie so richly on the surface. One of these is the word '*return*', which plays a major part in the book – naturally enough in view of the theme of God's reclaiming of His bride, first acted out in miniature in Hosea's home. Since it means not only 'return' but more basically 'turn', it can be either the very picture of desertion and estrangement, as one party turns their back upon the other,[2] or more happily, of renouncing such a course and turning to be reunited. So, in this better sense, it embraces both repentance and conversion, crowned with reconciliation. The word is as strong as it is simple.

---

[2] The noun from this verb is rendered at 11:7 'turning away' (RSV), 'rebellion' (NEB), *etc.*, and at 14:4 (5, Heb.) 'faithlessness' (RSV) or, better, 'apostasy' (NEB). With a very different motive God has just spoken in 5:15 of His turning and going away, to bring Israel to her senses.

Among other points in verses 1–3 we can note how '*he has torn*' (1) picks up the violent word of 5:14 (there translated 'rend', RSV, or 'maul', NEB) and how it sees, behind the trauma of invasion, not just the savagery of man but the judgment and discipline of God. The classic model of this constructive attitude to calamity, deserved or undeserved, is in Joseph's words, 'You meant evil against me; but God meant it for good' (Gn. 50:20).

Notice, again, how radical a cure is looked for. Bandaging and healing (1) provide one way of expressing it, but bringing back to life (2) does better justice to man's plight and to God's power. Admittedly the words 'revive' and 'live' need mean no more than 'heal' and 'recover'; but they can also and more properly express the meeting of a need as desperate as that which faced Ezekiel in the vision of his people as a heap of dry bones, or Paul in his diagnosis of man as 'dead in trespasses and sins' (Ezk. 37:1–14; Eph. 2:1). Nothing short of resurrection is fit to describe such need and such salvation; and while the mention of *the third day* would sound to Hosea's hearers as the mere equivalent of 'very soon', the prophet may have spoken more significantly than he knew;[3] for it is only in Christ's resurrection that His people are effectively raised up, as both Paul and Peter teach us.[4] And when Paul finds, apparently, not only the resurrection but even 'the third day' to be 'in accordance with the scriptures' (1 Cor. 15:4), it is at least possible – though one should put it no higher – that this passage as well as 'the sign of Jonah' was in his mind.

Then the call, *Let us know, let us press on to know the Lord* (3), lifts the appeal decisively above the plane of mere national survival, to that of a growing relationship with God.[5] This anticipates not only the climax of the great verse 6, 'the knowledge of God', but also our Lord's own definition of the content of eternal life, as to 'know thee the only true God, and Jesus Christ whom thou hast sent' (Jn. 17:3). It is, after all, a *marriage* that God is concerned with; nothing less. So the perseverance which the first line of the verse invites is more than matched from God's side, using the lovely metaphors of the unfailing sunrise[6] and the transforming rains.

[3] *Cf.* 1 Pet. 1:10–12.
[4] 1 Cor. 15:17; Eph. 2:5f.; 1 Pet. 1:3.
[5] *Cf.* Paul's ambition 'that I may know him', as he 'presses on' (Phil. 3:10–16).

After all this, the anticlimax of verse 4 is shattering – as heart-breaking, we may feel, as our own performance,

> 'For I forget so soon;
> The early dew of morning
> Has passed away at noon.'

Heart-breaking indeed; but met with neither a helpless wringing of hands nor a pointless flash of temper. The fierceness of verse 5, with its hewing and slaying, is not blind fury, but has the clarity of light, the purity of justice[7] and the constructiveness of love – for verse 6 reveals the end in view. Notice, too, the implied appeal to reason and conscience, for the 'hewing and slaying' was 'by the prophets' first of all. God does not send His judgments without warning or without the offer of repentance.

Verse 6 was a saying highly treasured by our Lord: see Matthew 9:13; 12:7. Like the two great commandments which He picked out as the ruling principles of the law, it pinpoints the supportive relationship to our fellows and the filial relationship to God that are the heart of true religion. It is a theme of all Hosea's great contemporaries, stirring them to some of their most powerful pronouncements: *e.g.*, Isaiah 1:12–17; Amos 5:21–24; Micah 6:6–8.

The rebuff to God's advances

6:7 *But at Adam they transgressed the covenant;*
there they dealt faithlessly with me.
8 *Gilead is a city of evildoers,*
tracked with blood
9 *As robbers lie in wait for a man,*
so the priests are banded together;

---

[6] The word for 'going forth' suits not only the idea of a person's setting out on a journey or an errand, but of the sun's majestic emergence to run its course: *cf.* Ps. 19:6 (7, Heb.).

[7] Verse 5c is a half-line, hence NEB transfers it to precede verse 3's half-line ('his going forth', *etc.*). But it has an important function in verse 5, whether as read in RSV ('my judgment', as in LXX, Syr.) or as in RSV mg. ('thy judgment', *i.e.*, 'thy justice', as in MT, anticipating Israel's chastened return to moral integrity).

they murder on the way to Shechem,
      yea, they commit villainy.
10 *In the house of Israel I have seen a horrible thing;*
      Ephraim's harlotry is there, Israel is defiled.

11 *For you also, O Judah, a harvest is appointed.*

    When I would restore the fortunes of my people,
7:1   *when I would heal Israel,*
    the corruption of Ephraim is revealed,
      and the wicked deeds of Samaria;
    for they deal falsely,
      the thief breaks in,
      and the bandits raid without.
  2 *But they do not consider*
      that I remember all their evil works.
    Now their deeds encompass them,
      they are before my face.

For all Hosea's highlighting of Israel's broken marriage and God's tenacious love, his prophecy is always well 'earthed', quick to expose the unromantic social cost of Israel's marital adventures. Here as ever the tragic and the squalid intertwine. Spiritually, there is the tragedy of her cast-off marriage vows (6:7) and of her 'harlotry' (10) in taking up with any customer – any pagan deity or cultic novelty – that comes along. Morally and socially, we see the squalor of a lawless society, with not only thieves and bandits spreading terror (7:1) but the very priests turning religion into a heartless, even murderous racket.[8] (Jesus was to find the same. Perhaps the church today can be grateful to be without the power that offers this temptation!)

The place-names in this passage would obviously waken embarrassing memories for Hosea's hearers, though we no

---

[8] The talk of 'murder on the way to Shechem' (6:9) may be a strong way of saying that the pilgrims lured to this paganized sanctuary go there to their spiritual destruction (see on 4:15). Or it may be literal, referring to some recent outrage or to a continuing vendetta. H. W. Wolff suggests, *e.g.*, that Shechem, far from being paganized, may have been too orthodox for the liking of its rival shrines, so that its pilgrims went in danger of their lives. We simply do not know enough.

longer have the clues to them. This hardly matters: in fact it emphasizes his concern – which is also God's – with what is very local, very topical, as well as with the wider sweep of history. As J.L. Mays has strikingly observed, '6:7–10 is a sort of miniature guidebook to the geography of sin in Israel; going from one place to another it catalogues the famous crimes of various localities as an indictment of the whole nation.'

In RSV and most modern versions (but not NIV), *Adam* is treated as the name of one of these towns, and the expression 'Like Adam' (6:7, 'Like Adam, they have broken the covenant') is taken to be an error for 'At Adam . . .'. There is no textual basis for this change, which seems to rob the verse of a powerful comparison (as, incidentally, RSV robs Jb. 31:33 of the same phrase for no good reason), but it must be admitted that the next line, '*there* they dealt faithlessly with me', is hard to account for if no place has yet been mentioned.[9]

The final verse in this section, as we have divided it at 7:2, is the most alarming of all, and it breathes a very modern atmosphere. People's bland dismissal of any question of divine judgment has made repentance virtually unthinkable. One is reminded of the veiled amusement with which (at the time of writing these comments) a leading broadcaster reported a local church's arrangement of a day of prayer for national repentance during a time of exceptional industrial bitterness. To him and, by implication, to the bulk of his hearers, God was laughably irrelevant. To God, by contrast, a people and its sins are anything but irrelevant. To paraphrase this verse, guilt does not fade with time; it wraps a people round; it stares God in the face.

Hosea 7:3–16
Decadence

Some of Hosea's most brilliant similes are clustered here, as he exposes the corruption of the palace, the nation, the diplomats

---

[9] A possible answer is that Hosea is speaking of a realm of behaviour, not a locality. *Cf.* G. A. F. Knight (*Torch Commentary*, 1960): 'THERE, in this very matter of keeping covenant . . .'. Those, however, who argue for a locality, point out (a) that Jos. 3:16 mentions a place named Adam, and (b) that the Heb. prefix *b* ('at') is easily confused with *k* ('like'), although the ancient versions agree with the Heb. text here against the modern emendation.

and even the prayers that people utter. But he is not scoring points. God's concern is that of a father for a son who refuses to be helped. This revealing relationship, mentioned in passing in verse 15, will be taken up again and sensitively explored in chapter 11.

Corruption at court

7:3 *By their wickedness they make the king glad,*
and the princes by their treachery.
4 *They are all adulterers;*
they are like a heated oven,
whose baker ceases to stir the fire,
from the kneading of the dough until it is leavened.
5 *On the day of our king the princes*
became sick with the heat of wine;
he stretched out his hand with mockers.
6 *For like an oven their hearts burn with intrigue;*
all night their anger smoulders;
in the morning it blazes like a flaming fire.
7 *All of them are hot as an oven,*
and they devour their rulers.
All their kings have fallen;
and none of them calls upon me.

This lurid scene is the culmination of the previous section, which brought us from the country towns to Samaria, the capital. Now we penetrate the palace, to find the king and his courtiers not only doing nothing to stem the tide of evil, but revelling in it, titillated by it, relishing the prevailing graft and trickery (3), and letting their lusts take over. The picture of the oven that needs no stoking once the fermentation has begun, tells its own story of self-propagating passion – but Hosea will give a further twist to this simile before he finishes.

The royal anniversary (5) should have had the stamp of greatness on it, rising to the vision of such a psalm as 72:

Give the king thy justice, O God,
and thy righteousness to the royal son! . . .
May he be like rain that falls on the mown grass,
like showers that water the earth!

In his days may righteousness flourish,
and peace abound, till the moon be no more!
(Ps. 72:1, 6–7)

Instead, it was an orgy. In a few biting phrases Hosea evokes the scene for us, with its sprawling, flushed and ribald fools: a scene repeated often enough where boasters (from Ben-hadad, 'drinking himself drunk' before a battle, to the doomed Belshazzar, drinking toasts to his gods from the temple vessels), and escapists like these 'vain and light persons', try to transcend themselves with the help of what they swallow. Amos at about this time was encountering the same flight from reality, conducted admittedly with more finesse, among the dilettanti of Israel and Judah; but Isaiah paints an even more revolting picture than Hosea's of the kind of party that we find here – and in his oracle the chief revellers are, of all people, priests and prophets.[1]

Now (reverting to Hosea's simile) the banked-up fire of verse 4, that pleasurable build-up of shared lust, bursts into a frightening blaze, as passions flare not merely into lechery (as in verse 4) but into murder (6–7) – for when passion reigns there are no limits or loyalties. With such a fever running at every level of society, it was no coincidence that Israel's last three decades were a turmoil of intrigue, as one conspirator after another hacked his way to the throne, only to be murdered in his turn. Of the six men who reigned in those thirty years, four were assassins, and only one died in his own bed.[2]

A nation of unteachables

7:8 *Ephraim mixes himself with the peoples;*
Ephraim is a cake not turned.
9 *Aliens devour his strength,*
and he knows it not;
grey hairs are sprinkled upon him,
and he knows it not.
10 *The pride of Israel witnesses against him;*
yet they do not return to the Lord their God,
nor seek him, for all this.

[1] See Am. 6:1–7; Is. 28:7ff.
[2] The last king, Hoshea, may have escaped a violent end, but he died in captivity. The four assassinations are recorded in 2 Ki. 15:10, 14, 25 and 30.

11 *Ephraim is like a dove,*
   silly and without sense,
   calling to Egypt, going to Assyria.
12 *As they go, I will spread over them my net;*
   I will bring them down like birds of the air;
   I will chastise them for their wicked deeds.
13 *Woe to them, for they have strayed from me!*
   Destruction to them, for they have rebelled against me!
I would redeem them,
   but they speak lies against me.

14 *They do not cry to me from the heart,*
   but they wail upon their beds;
for grain and wine they gash themselves,
   they rebel against me.
15 *Although I trained and strengthened their arms,*
   yet they devise evil against me.
16 *They turn to Baal;*
   they are like a treacherous bow,
their princes shall fall by the sword
   because of the insolence of their tongue.
This shall be their derision in the land of Egypt.

It is one scathing picture after another: the inedible cake, the first grey hairs, the flustered bird, the flawed weapon. Poor Israel! Poor church, perhaps?

It may be gilding the lily to add anything to these vignettes, but each of them has more content than a first glance may take in.

On the first of them (8) George Adam Smith has been quoted again and again, but his comment deserves it: 'How better describe a half-fed people, a half-cultured society, a half-lived religion, a half-hearted policy, than by a half-baked scone?'[3] The first line of this couplet, 'Ephraim mixes himself with the peoples', brings out the loss of conviction which left this people neither one thing nor the other: neither a light to the Gentiles nor an excusable product of paganism. The church in every age

---

[3] Smith, p. 273. The flat cake in question would be of dough baked either on hot stones or pressed against the side of an oven. Not turned over, one side would be burnt, the other uncooked. Was this a memory from the stormy marriage?

knows this temptation, and tends to meet it either by retreat into itself or by melting into its surroundings. The gospels demonstrate a better way in their account of the good physician and the friend of sinners: wholly Himself yet wholly accessible, and as compassionate as He was uncompromising.

The second figure, of the man who thinks himself still in his prime (9), may recall to us (in muted terms) the plight of Samson, his strength devoured by the aliens whom he loved and hated, while 'he did not know that the Lord had left him' (Jdg. 16:20). For Israel there has been as yet no rude awakening like his. To this people, if not to others, the decline is doubly imperceptible, unnoticed through its gradualness and invisible to their pride. Yet the pride itself is a tell-tale sign of it – almost like the hardening lines in a face[4] – and a fatal obstacle to their even considering repentance. We noticed at 5:4–5 the inhibiting influence of the sinner's cherished ways and attitudes. The repetition here of 5:5a ('the pride of Israel testifies to his face') draws attention to the most damning and also most addictive of sin's ingredients. The victim, as our verse 10 sadly observes, would rather not be helped.

The third simile, the frantic dove (11–12), lends a cartoonist's wit and verve to a theme already touched on at 5:13, one which will reappear at intervals from now on. To put it prosaically, the theme is Israel's diplomatic duplicity, for she kept faith with no-one, least of all with God, but changed alliances with every shift of the political wind. We saw how King Menahem bought Assyria's patronage.[5] His son's assassin, Pekah, went back on this alignment as soon as it ceased to suit him – and lost half his kingdom.[6] His successor, Hoshea, followed his example and lost the rest – for after renewing the allegiance he broke it by intrigue with Egypt, only to lose what little remained of his realm for ever (2 Ki. 17:1–6).

All this was 'silly and without sense'; but it was worse: it was desertion and rebellion – and not only politically but, as God says in verse 13, 'from *me*', 'against *me*'. This is the dimension the opportunist always forgets. So the darting diplomats, flit-

---

[4] One could even translate 10a 'the pride of Israel shows (lit. 'answers', as in a mirror) in his face'.

[5] 2 Ki. 15:19. See above, p. 62.

[6] 2 Ki. 15:29. In 2 Ki. 16:5ff. and Is. 7:1ff. we read of Pekah's alliance with Syria and his attempt to force Judah into an anti-Assyrian league.

ting from patron to patron like birds from tree to tree, were to fly straight into the one peril they had overlooked: the net of divine judgment. Yet characteristically Hosea gives us not only the sentence that must be passed on them, but God's rueful comment on it:

> I would redeem them,
>   but they speak lies against me.

For what can even God do for the insincere? We get a glimpse in verse 14 of their kind of praying ('Never mind about "Thy kingdom come" – where's our daily bread?'). It was all self-pity and piling on the pressure by self-mutilation, more like the blackmail of a child's tantrum than a genuine heart-cry. That was how one prayed to Baal,[7] not to the Lord; and whether or not the actual name of Baal should occur in verse 16,[8] God reads it at least between the lines, and is as hurt as He is angry. To rebel (14c) is bad enough, but what the Lord repeatedly points out through Hosea (a prophet sensitized to this through his own unhappy past) is that they are sinning against love. It was a husband's love in chapter 2; but now, and supremely in chapter 11, it is a father's, with a glimpse in verse 15a of that tenderness, care and pride with which this father has sought to make a man of his son Israel.

The chapter ends bleakly. Its threat of 'sword' and 'derision' is not arbitrary. To betray and belittle everything to which one owes most (notice 'the insolence of their tongue', 16) is a sure mark of decadence; and decadence is an invitation to the predator. It is also cynicism, and the cynical get the friends they deserve, who are sure to find their plight merely amusing (16b).

We are left, too, with the fourth of this chapter's scathing

[7] *Cf.* 1 Ki. 18:28, if 'gash', rather than 'gather', is the right reading in our verse 14, as LXX and some Heb. MSS suggest. The letters *d* and *r*, on which the textual question pivots, are closely alike in Hebrew.

[8] The Heb. text has 'They turn not upward' (*lō' 'āl*), an unusual expression both in word-order and in meaning (since *'al* is normally a preposition, 'on', 'over', *etc.*). Most modern versions therefore assume a copying error for *l^eba'al*, 'to Baal' (but see NIV). Yet the modern name El Al ('to the height'), adopted by the Israelis for their airline, is a reminder that a noun ('height') underlies the preposition; and indeed *'el 'al* occurs in the Heb. of 11:7, where see note. On balance, however, the conjectured reading, 'to Baal', seems the most likely.

pictures: the flawed weapon of verse 16a. (For the others, see the first remarks on this section, pp. 72ff.) It is perhaps the most serious of the four, for a weapon may imply a life-and-death situation, in which its failure spells the end of everything. And this 'treacherous bow' is not merely weak: it is warped, as the context of 'lies' and 'devising evil' makes clear. Psalm 78:57 puts it well:

(They) turned away and acted treacherously like their fathers;
    they *twisted* like a deceitful bow.

✻   ✻   ✻

O Lord, grant us grace never to parley with temptation,
never to tamper with conscience, never to spare the right eye,
or hand, or foot that is a snare to us;
never to lose our souls, though in exchange we should gain
the whole world.

(Christina Rossetti)

Hosea 8:1–14
Sowing the wind, reaping the whirlwind

If there is one theme that unifies the diversity of this chapter, it is that of Israel's dangerous self-reliance, with its self-appointed kings, its man-made calf, its expensive allies, its own version of religion, and its impressive fortresses. What God makes of all this, and what kind of test it could survive, these people have not troubled to ask themselves.

Alarmist or realist?

8:1 *Set the trumpet to your lips,*
    for a vulture is over the house of the Lord,
  because they have broken my covenant,
    and transgressed my law.
 2 *To me they cry,*
    My God, we Israel know thee.
 3 *Israel has spurned the good;*
    the enemy shall pursue him.

If no-one in Hosea's day, gazing complacently at the house or household of the Lord (like the disciples admiring the temple in Mt. 24:1), had noticed the ominous speck in the sky above it, it was high time someone pointed it out. The vulture[1] might not have long to wait; the object of its interest, the ailing nation, had even less. Its plight was nearly too late to mend. The Hebrew of verse 1 raps out the command in three words: 'Trumpet to your-lips!'

Yet nobody could quite believe it. We sense their mood as the chapter unfolds. 'Yes, times are bad, but surely not desperate! Another coup – who knows? – may bring the right man to the top. Abroad, we are bidding high for allies. Religion? There at least we are strong. Defence? We have a fine building programme. Let's at least be cheerful!' (*cf.* 9:1).

The cry of verse 2, 'We, Israel, know thee', has the double reliance on birth and breeding which would show itself again in the Jews' disputes with Jesus. 'We are descendants of Abraham'; 'We are disciples of Moses. *We know* ...' (Jn. 8:33; 9:28f.). The divine reply is virtually the same in both instances: your actions drown your words.[2] And in case we point the finger too easily at proud Israelites and Jews, the same test is applied to us: 'He who says "I know him" but disobeys his commandments is a liar' (1 Jn. 2:4).

What may seem at first merely repetitive in the triple accusation of verses 1–3 is in fact triply devastating, for the '*covenant*' spoke of the basic relationship with God – as binding and as intimate as marriage; the '*law*' spelt out the ways in which alone that partnership could be harmonious; and '*the good*' covers not only all this but everything that conscience and plain decency demand, or even that common sense suggests – for 'good' is by definition not only what is worth doing but what is worth having and worth being. To spurn this is to fall for a bargain that is no bargain – to 'spend' (as Is. 55:2 has put it)

[1] There is a slight query over this word, which is qualified by the particle 'as' (see RV mg.). On the basis of an Arabic word of similar consonants, Grace Emmerson offers the translation, '... lips, as a herald [making a proclamation] against the house of the Lord' (*VT* 25 (1975), pp 700–710). But the expression, lit. 'as-a-vulture', can be defended as indicating that the prophet is not speaking literally: *cf.* the repetitions of 'as it were' (the same particle) in Ezk. 1:26f.

[2] See, *e.g.*, Jn. 8:39–44, 55.

... 'your money for that which is not bread,
and your labour for that which does not satisfy'

and, we might add, 'your life for certain death'.

The self-help that is no help

The rest of the chapter pursues the theme launched in the first word of verse 4: 'They made kings ...' – for the Hebrew makes the 'They' emphatic here. Everything that follows has this pattern of 'They ... but not through me', whether it is politics, religion, diplomacy or defence.

a. Puppet kings and puppet gods

8:4 *They made kings, but not through me.*
 They set up princes, but without my knowledge.
With their silver and gold they made idols
 for their own destruction.
 5 *I have spurned your calf, O Samaria.*
 My anger burns against them.
How long will it be
 till they are pure ⁶ *in Israel?*

 A workman made it;
 it is not God.
The calf of Samaria
 shall be broken to pieces.

The classic comment on 'not through me' and 'without my knowledge' (*i.e.*, my recognition) is Psalm 127: 'Unless the Lord builds the house, ... Unless the Lord watches over the city ... It is in vain.' This disastrous king-making was part of a long series in Scripture, starting as far back as Abimelech, that 'bramble' only fit to start a forest fire (Jdg. 9:15), and reaching its spiritual climax in the cry, 'Not this man, but Barabbas!' (Jn. 18:40). That cry is echoed wherever the voice of the people (our vaunted democracy) drowns the voice of God; where we set up leaders and régimes supposedly answerable only to ourselves; where we treat even the moral law as subject to the vote or to the climate of opinion.

Although the king-making castigated here was far from democratic in our sense – being a series of conspiracies and bloody coups[3] – God saw it as the people's doing for all that; for the violence at the top had its roots in the anarchy below. We could have guessed as much, but chapter 4:1–3 has already put it beyond doubt.

Next, the puppet gods. The golden calf, or young bull, as a man-made god, had an even longer past for Israel than the man-made king. Its famous first appearance was, outrageously, at the foot of Mount Sinai itself and at the instigation of the future high priest, Aaron (Ex. 32:1ff.). (Perhaps by now we should be less surprised than Moses, though no less scandalized, at the high patronage that heresy has a way of securing from time to time.) Later, just after Solomon, Jeroboam I set up two golden calves, one at Bethel and one at Dan, as rallying-points for his breakaway kingdom of the north, Hosea's native land, as counter-attractions to the temple at Jerusalem (1 Ki. 12:27–30).

To us, a golden calf may seem completely unconvincing. But an accepted superstition, rather like an established point of etiquette, can put almost anything beyond challenge, by-passing reason even when reason utterly explodes it, as Hosea's argument does here.[4] In addition, though, it probably reflected an element of pagan thinking, since a bull is an obvious symbol of brute strength and sexual potency – qualities which a corrupt society tends to idolize. In that case, ancient Israel and Canaan may be closer to us than we suppose.

There is a telling link between verses 3 and 5 in the strong word *spurned*:

> Israel has spurned the good; . . .
> I have spurned your calf, O Samaria

– although the RSV (as above) has trimmed the second of these

---

[3] See above, pp. 70f.

[4] W. F. Albright's contention (*From the Stone Age to Christianity*, Doubleday Anchor Books, 1957, p. 299) that the calf was regarded as a mere pedestal for the invisible Yahweh (an idea based on Canaanite representations of the storm-god standing on a bull), would make the argument of verse 6 quite pointless. But Hosea knew his countrymen's beliefs too well to waste irrelevant ammunition on them. Clearly they were treating the calves as divine. *Cf.* 13:2.

from a literal 'he has' to 'I have', to make a smoother fit with the surrounding 'me' and 'my'. Either way, it is a sharp reminder that our lordly choices are not the last word in any situation. There is another will, another verdict, to be reckoned with.

But it may be an appeal: 'Spurn your calf, O Samaria'[5] – for there is once again a divine yearning in verse 5 ('How long . . . ?') mingled with the anger.

b. Desperate diplomacy

8:7 For they sow the wind,
    and they shall reap the whirlwind.
The standing grain has no heads,
    it shall yield no meal;
if it were to yield,
    aliens would devour it.
8 Israel is swallowed up;
    already they are among the nations
    as a useless vessel.
9 For they have gone up to Assyria,
    a wild ass wandering alone;
    Ephraim has hired lovers.
10 Though they hire allies among the nations,
    I will soon gather them up.
And they shall cease for a little while
    from anointing king and princes.[6]

'Sow the wind, . . . reap the whirlwind' has become so much a part of our language that we may miss the surprise of it here. Hearing it for the first time, we should expect the reaping to be simply negative: 'put nothing in, and you'll get nothing out.' Instead, the harvest is positive disaster, as in Paul's sequence: 'he who sows to his own flesh will from the flesh reap' – not disappointment, but 'corruption' (Gal. 6:8) – for there are no half-measures in the end.

[5] Cf. NIV, following LXX, reading the existing consonants with a shortened first vowel. (NEB opts for a similar but rare verb, 'to stink', in both verses – a more precarious translation.)

[6] In verse 10b RSV (as above) follows LXX. The NIV (cf. also RV) is preferable here in retaining the Massoretic Text, which it renders, 'They will begin to waste away under the oppression of the mighty king' (lit. ' a king of princes').

The main context here is foreign policy, but the main issue is faith – and fidelity. As the last chapter showed (7:11ff.), Israel was gambling on one hunch after another, forever changing sides and (as our verse 10 points out) desperately bidding for influential friendships. This way she would win only distrust and scorn as a 'useless vessel', or as JB puts it, 'a crock that no one wants'; and in the end she would reap the terrible fate of a traitor. So the metaphorical harvest – the whirlwind of judgment – would be accompanied by quite literally empty fields, either as the fertility cult of Baal failed its devotees (see verse 7a, b, with 2:5, 9), or as the punitive armies stripped the land (7c).

The lesson needs no spiritualizing to bring it to our doorstep. Certainly it is valid at the spiritual level, as Galatians 6 points out, for false religion pays disastrous dividends. But guile and duplicity in any field, political, commercial or personal, are equally perilous tactics to adopt. Dabbling in evil, we may be amateurs; but we are playing with professionals who will make short work of us, as we are warned not only in the well-known saying of Ephesians 6:12 but in the detailed admonitions that lead up to it from Ephesians 4:25 onwards.

c. Religiosity

8:11 *Because Ephraim has multiplied altars for sinning,*
    they have become to him altars for sinning.
12 *Were I to write for him my laws by ten thousands,*
    they would be regarded as a strange thing.
13 *They love sacrifice;*
    they sacrifice flesh and eat it;
    but the Lord has no delight in them.
Now he will remember their iniquity,
    and punish their sins;
    they shall return to Egypt.

The first two lines of this read so oddly, as they stand, that most modern versions have taken a fresh look at the Hebrew consonants to see if they will yield a better meaning. (The original text, like modern Hebrew, left the reader to supply the vowels.) The NIV (*cf.* GNB) offers as good a solution as any, keeping the consonants unchanged but pronouncing them so as to read: '... altars for sin offerings ... have become altars for sinning'.[7]

This chimes in forcefully with verse 13 and with the protests of Hosea's contemporaries, Amos, Micah and Isaiah.[8] Paul had to warn us of something very similar (1 Cor. 11:27). It seems to be an occupational disease of worshippers to think more of the mechanics than the meaning of what we do; more of getting it right than of getting ourselves right; and this can degenerate from thoughtlessness into something worse, ranging from cynical detachment, if we are sophisticated, to religious superstition if we are not. What the prophets show us is heaven's strong reaction to such attitudes: that this parody of worship is not simply valueless, as we might have guessed, but insulting and even sickening to God, attracting the very judgment it is supposed to avert. This is the irony that runs throughout this paragraph. It is put more vehemently still in the invective of Isaiah and Amos, in the passages we have footnoted, and above all in the shuddering words of Christ to lukewarm Laodicea (Rev. 3:16).

The gulf between such worshippers and God is seen at its widest in verse 12. There is no meeting of minds, divine and human; still less of wills. This verse, incidentally, has been a talking-point between critical scholars, on the question of how much or little of God's law was in writing in Hosea's day;[9] but its real aim is to show how deaf to all appeal and all correction God's people have become. However much He says, and however plainly (for it is given as written law), it will be treated as an irrelevance or a kind of incantation, while the services and sacraments (as in 13a) continue and proliferate. The New Testament reports the same shutting of the mind to the gospel

---

[7] *I.e.*, reading the intensive (Pi'el) form of 'to sin' in 11a, and the non-intensive (Qal) in 11b. The Pi'el form means to make a sin-offering; the Qal, using the same consonants, means to sin. (Note that English, like Hebrew, sometimes uses the same verb to mean either the doing or the undoing of a thing: *e.g.*, we 'dust' an object with a powder, or dust it clean; and so on.)

[8] *E.g.*, Am. 5:21ff.; Mi. 6:6ff.; Is. 1:11ff.

[9] On their own showing, God's laws had been in writing since the days of Moses (Ex. 24:3–7; Dt. 31:24–26). If confirmation were needed, the AV of Ho. 8:12 ('I have written ...') would seem to supply it (*cf.* NIV), but the Heb. construction tends to favour a hypothetical statement, as in RSV, *etc.*, or a present tense: 'I write down countless teachings' (GNB; *cf.* NEB).

as to the law, [10] and reveals the source, deep in our fallen nature, of this deafness to the voice of God:

'The natural man receiveth not the things of the Spirit of God: for they are foolishness unto him: neither can he know them, because they are spiritually discerned' (1 Cor. 2:14, AV).

In the threat, 'they shall return to Egypt' (13), perhaps the deepest thrust lies in the word 'return'. Was *this* to be the end of their great epic, the exodus? Elsewhere Assyria is coupled with Egypt as their place of exile, and Assyria was in fact to be their conqueror and captor; so Egypt probably received only refugees. Yet this word 'return' is used in 9:3 and 11:5 as well as here, for they had spiritually retraced their steps to Egypt long before they did so physically. It stands in pointed contrast to the couplet of 11:1,

> When Israel was a child, I loved him,
> and out of Egypt I called my son.

Even so, the last word would be with grace, not judgment:

> They shall come trembling like birds from Egypt,
> and like doves from the land of Assyria
> (Ho. 11:11).

In these and other references to their oldest captivity, the pattern of the book, as *grace – disgrace – grace abounding*, comes out once more.

d. Misplaced trust

8:14 *For Israel has forgotten his Maker,*
and built palaces;
and Judah has multiplied fortified cities;
but I will send a fire upon his cities,
and it shall devour his strongholds.

The first sentence of this is the key to it, for the Old Testament

---

[10] *E.g.* Mt. 13:13ff. and parallels; Jn. 12:37ff.; Acts 28:25ff.

does not despise fine buildings or strong walls (*cf*. Ps. 48:12f., but 14): only the notion that they are in themselves fit to be one's glory[11] or security. Nehemiah, building his wall and carefully deploying his little work-force, showed the right priorities in his order of the day: '... *Remember the Lord*, who is great and terrible, and fight for your brethren, your sons, your daughters, your wives, and your homes' (Ne. 4:14).

As for Judah's 'fortified cities', the brutal answer to them was only a generation away. There were forty-six of them, according to Sennacherib, and their fate is told in a single verse of 2 Kings. 'In the fourteenth year of King Hezekiah Sennacherib king of Assyria came up against all the fortified cities of Judah and took them' (2 Ki. 18:13). The only one to survive was Jerusalem, following the message from God to Hezekiah which opened with the significant words: 'Your prayer to me about Sennacherib king of Assyria I have heard' (2 Ki. 19:20).

Hosea 9:1–17
Wanderers among the nations

The sentencing of Israel to a wandering existence, in the final verse, will round off a chapter which has fully paved the way to it. This people has been restless enough, ogling one nation after another; heedless enough, dismissing as madmen its look-out men, the prophets; fickle enough, forsaking the Lord for Baal even from the days of Moses. Hosea will increasingly draw on history in the next few chapters, chiefly with passing allusions, to show how well-earned are the judgments he is having to pronounce from God.

The party is over

9:1 *Rejoice not, O Israel!*
Exult not like the peoples;
for you have played the harlot, forsaking your God.
You have loved a harlot's hire
upon all threshing floors.
2 *Threshing floor and winevat shall not feed them,*
and the new wine shall fail them.

[11] See the scathing comment on Jehoiakim's palace in Je. 22:13–17.

3 *They shall not remain in the land of the Lord;*
    but Ephraim shall return to Egypt,
    and they shall eat unclean food in Assyria.

4 *They shall not pour libations of wine to the Lord;*
    and they shall not please him with their sacrifices.
Their bread shall be like mourners' bread;
    all who eat of it shall be defiled;
for their bread shall be for their hunger only;
    it shall not come to the house of the Lord.

5 *What will you do on the day of appointed festival,*
    and on the day of the feast of the Lord?
6 *For behold, they are going to Assyria;*[1]
    Egypt shall gather them,
    Memphis shall bury them.
Nettles shall possess their precious things of silver;
    thorns shall be in their tents.

To us in our secular age it may seem odd that God should expect *religious* warnings to have much impact on a set of people as far gone in sin as Israel was. 'Nettles' submerging their treasures, yes; and 'thorns' taking over their deserted dwellings (6): these were a prospect to shake the most hardened. But ritually forbidden food (3c)? Cessation of sacrifice (4)? No pilgrimages (5)? How could these be matters for dismay?

The clue is in the previous chapter, 8:12–13; above all in chapter 2. Religion, to them, penetrated everything except the conscience. It was a charm against trouble, a compelling pattern of festivals, stories, customs and taboos that gave shape to life; and with its heady Canaanite embellishments it could have the excitement of an orgy. It also gave you an identity: you, your people, your traditions, your native soil and the God or gods who presided over your land, all these were a close-knit structure whose disintegration would leave you totally adrift.

The one thing missing was the very heart of true religion, the loyal love that alone could make God's covenant-partner a true wife to Him. As it was, His will held not the slightest interest

---

[1] RSV modifies the Heb. of this line (*cf.* RSV mg.), which contains no reference to Assyria. It should be translated as in, *e.g.*, NIV, 'Even if they escape from destruction, Egypt shall gather them,' *etc.*

for her, as 8:12 showed; her only loyalty was to her appetites. The harsh word 'harlot' (1) was no exaggeration. And in case our interest in the portrait should be only academic, as if it were applicable solely to ancient idolaters or, at most, modern renegades, the New Testament startles us with a similar outburst in James 4:4 against mere worldliness – calling us in that case 'adulteresses', although some modern versions have put it more politely.

Israel's judgment would be all too fitting. For her political flirtations she would have her fill of foreign loves, her people captive in Assyria and fugitives in Egypt.[2] For her religious flirtations, too, she would pay the proper price of having scattered her favours everywhere: her people ending up with nothing fit to offer God, and nowhere to hold their beloved festivals.[3]

'The prophet is a fool'

9:7 *The days of punishment have come,*
        the days of recompense have come;
        Israel shall know it.
    The prophet is a fool,
        the man of the spirit is mad,
    because of your great iniquity
        and great hatred.
  8 *The prophet is the watchman of Ephraim,*
        the people of my God,
    yet a fowler's snare is on all his ways,
        and hatred in the house of his God.
  9 *They have deeply corrupted themselves*
        as in the days of Gibeah:
    he will remember their iniquity,
        he will punish their sins.

[2] See verse 3, and the comment on 'they shall return to Egypt' at 8:13. As to their return there as fugitives, see the footnote to the text of verse 6, above.

[3] The point of the comparison with 'mourners' bread' is not that one ate forbidden food on such occasions, but that mourning rites made one technically unclean by their association with death; and it was sacrilege to partake of holy things while so disqualified (see Dt. 26:14; Lv. 7:21). Just so, the defilement of heathen Assyria would cling to them all the time that they were there under judgment.

When disembodied fingers wrote an unintelligible message at Belshazzar's feast, the king was sobered at once, and desperate for an answer (Dn. 5:5ff.). But when a man of God spoke intelligibly and with passion to his own people, he was 'a fool' and 'mad' (7). He was not the first or last to be called this. 'Why did this mad fellow come to you?' was the reaction of Jehu's friends to a prophet's visit; and Jeremiah was named in a letter which urged the authorities to put 'every madman who prophesies ... in the stocks and collar'.[4] Paul was to be paid the same compliment by Festus (Acts 26:24), and our Lord was accused of being demon-possessed (Jn. 7:20; 8:48).

Jesus told us to expect and welcome a prophet's persecution and misrepresentation (Mt. 5:12); and here verse 8b gives a sample of such treatment in the attempts to entangle and compromise the speaker ('the fowler's snare') and in the special venom of religious disdain ('hatred in the house of his God'). What Hosea lets us glimpse in this single sentence, Jeremiah reveals to us at length, recording the threats to his life by his fellow villagers (Je. 11:19, 21), the taunts and whisperings (Je. 17:15ff.; 20:10), the isolation: 'I sat alone, because thy hand was upon me' (Je. 15:17). But God, in our passage, has a better name than 'fool' for such a man. 'The prophet is the *watchman*' (8) – a calling whose implications can be studied in some detail in Ezekiel 33:1–9.

While rejection is a prophet's honour, it is a people's doom. This judgment is expressed impersonally at the beginning of this paragraph (7a), as a due process of law ('punishment') and a settling of accounts ('recompense', RSV; 'reckoning', NIV), but in personal terms in the closing statement (9b), where the Lord Himself exacts the penalty. These two aspects of judgment, as the inexorable logic of events and as the act of God in person, are held together in Scripture. The couplet,

> he will remember their iniquity,
> he will punish their sins,

---

[4] See 2 Ki. 9:11; Je. 29:26f. The epithet may have originated from the excited or ecstatic behaviour of some of the early prophets, true and false: *cf.. e.g.*, 1 Sa. 18:10 (where 'raved', RSV, = 'prophesied', AV); *cf.* 19:24; 1 Ki. 18:29. But it became a convenient way of dismissing an unwelcome prophecy, as Je. 29:24ff. shows, since the writer of the letter against Jeremiah was himself a self-styled prophet.

is the dark alternative to the grace of the new covenant, which is equally personal:

> I will forgive their iniquity,
> and I will remember their sin no more
> (Je. 31:34).

There is no middle way, and no side-stepping of repentance if grace is to prevail.

As for the depth of Israel's guilt, the mere mention of *Gibeah* (9) is measurement enough, for its story in Judges 19–21 leaves Sodom and Gomorrah with nothing they could teach this city, whose depravity at that period was only equalled by its arrogance in brazening the matter out. It would have wholly approved of today's re-naming of sodomy as the gay life. For a fuller treatment of such moral value reversals we have Paul's study in Romans 1:18–32, where his final comment (32) could as readily have arisen from an encounter with our present society as with his own or with Hosea's.

The glory departs

9:10 *Like grapes in the wilderness,*
> *I found Israel.*
Like the first fruit on the fig tree,
> *in its first season,*
> *I saw your fathers.*
But they came to Baal-peor,
> *and consecrated themselves to Baal,*
> *and became detestable like the thing they loved.*
11 *Ephraim's glory shall fly away like a bird –*
> *no birth, no pregnancy, no conception!*
12 *Even if they bring up children,*
> *I will bereave them till none is left.*
Woe to them
> *when I depart from them!*
13 *Ephraim's sons, as I have seen, are destined for a prey;*
> *Ephraim must lead forth his sons to slaughter.*
14 *Give them, O Lord –*
> *what wilt thou give?*
Give them a miscarrying womb
> *and dry breasts.*

Delight and anticipation could hardly be more vividly expressed than in this opening reminiscence of the Lord's great early venture with His people. Allowing for its language of manlike relish and dreamlike anomaly – 'grapes in the wilderness'! – the passage conveys something which our careful theology cannot quite pin down: the Lord's zest and enjoyment, so different from cold charity, in His encounters with responsive love, however meagre that response may be.

It makes the shock of disappointment all the stronger – and this again is something which our consciousness of divine foreknowledge and of measured wrath may hide from us. But in the gospels the echo of verse 10a in the incident of the barren fig tree, so eagerly approached at a moment of hunger (Mt. 21:18ff.), makes the same point about God and man, at whatever risk of pricking us into high-minded protest.

The story of Baal-peor (10b), which can be read in Numbers 25, is very apt, since it combined the two kinds of unchastity which Hosea had to fight: the physical and the spiritual. It was not only the Moabite women but their local Baal that had seduced the men of the exodus; and we have already heard Hosea's protests against the same two levels of adultery in his day.[5] We might add that in our own day the virtual worshipping of sex, needing no Baal to make it a religion, has proved as potent a distraction as it did in Old Testament times. Incidentally Hosea is not being merely rhetorical when he calls apostates 'destestable like the thing they loved'. Using a standard term for idols, *viz.*, 'abominations' (RSV 'detestable' here), he points out that what you give yourself to, you not only come to resemble (Ps. 115:8), but you make common cause with it. If it is an abomination to God, so, appallingly, are you; if its second name is 'shame',[6] so is yours.

What follows from this allusion to Baal-peor and the surrender to lust is not a set of arbitrary punishments but the end-products of so squalid and treacherous a choice. The quickest thing to disappear, when this fever grips a people, is *glory* (11) – whether in the sense of self-respect (for conscience must be silenced by cynicism), or of reputation, or, more profoundly, of the glory of God's presence. A nation may be

[5] *E.g.* Ho. 2:13; 4:14.
[6] The second occurrence of 'Baal' in verse 10 (RSV) is in the Heb. text 'Bosheth', *i.e.* 'shame', a frequent substitute for his name in the Old Testament.

spiritless enough to shrug off the loss of glory, but what is left 'when I (the Lord) depart from them' (12)? The name Ichabod marked such a moment, or so at least it seemed, in an earlier generation, when the ark of God was captured (1 Sa. 4:21); and Ezekiel would later have a vision of God's glory withdrawing from Jerusalem (Ezk. 8:6; 11:23). For our comfort we can remember the sequel to that capture and, in Ezekiel 43:2ff., to that withdrawal; but the people whom Hosea was addressing would soon be losing not only their glory but their corporate identity as the northern kingdom, for ever.

But whether or not they cared about the loss of glory or of God, there was another and more tangible loss to face. From verse 11 to the end of the chapter the family tree of Ephraim (that is, of the northern tribes) is seen either dying back or being lopped of all new growth. They have worshipped fertility through the sex-rites of Baal, and they have sold their souls for peace:[7] their judgment will be infertility and war. Here again it is a blend of natural and supernatural processes: natural, in that in any case the abuse of sex tends towards disease and to the barrenness of 11b and 14, and that broken treaties tend to leave a country friendless (12–13);[8] but supernatural in that God will see this matter through to the bitter end.

The disinherited

9:15 *Every evil of theirs is in Gilgal;*
    there I began to hate them.
  Because of the wickedness of their deeds
    I will drive them out of my house.
  I will love them no more;
    all their princes are rebels.

16 *Ephraim is stricken,*
    their root is dried up,
    they shall bear no fruit.
  Even though they bring forth,
    I will slay their beloved children.

[7] See, e.g., 7:11; 8:9f.

[8] RSV and most modern versions follow LXX in 13a, but the Heb. text is as in RV (cf. AV, NIV): 'Ephraim, like as I have seen Tyre, is planted in a pleasant place: but . . .'.

17   *My God will cast them off,*
      because they have not hearkened to him;
      they shall be wanderers among the nations.

Every nation has its celebrated spots, whose names evoke the glories of the past or present. Yet sometimes it might be startling to compare their earthly with their heavenly reputations. Gilgal is a case in point: hallowed by its altars (12:11) and its famous names and moments (Joshua's first foothold in the promised land, Saul's first kingly glory, David's welcome back from exile[9]) – all of which leave God entirely unimpressed. Far from hallowed, it is crammed with evil; and the only reference to its history (if such it is in verse 15a) is to its role in forfeiting God's favour for the nation as a whole.

In its direct, outspoken way this is as devastating as Amos's barbed mockery of its corrupted shrine and superstitious pilgrims:

> Go to Bethel and sin;
>   go to Gilgal and sin yet more.[10]

But what is meant by 'there I began to hate them'? 'Hate' is a harsh Hebrew way of expressing rejection, used with varying degrees of severity and emotional content.[11] The warm affection which pervades this book from end to end (see, *e.g.*, 3:1b; 11:1ff.; 14:4) forbids us to take either 'I began to hate them' or 'I will love them no more' (15) as expressions of mere animosity. Rather this language is announcing (with what anguish, other passages make evident: *e.g.* 6:4; 11:8) a break-off of relations which amounts to the suspension of the marriage ('I will drive them out of my house', 15) as the only hope of mending it. The theme has already met us in the sequence of severity and tenderness in 2:2ff. with 2:14ff. and in the last verse of chapter 5.

Incidentally the RSV is somewhat misleading here, since the

---

[9] Jos. 4:19; 1 Sa. 11:14f.; 2 Sa. 19:15.
[10] Am. 4:4, NIV.
[11] The discipleship sayings, *e.g.* Lk. 14:26, are at one extreme, and that of 1 Jn. 3:15 at the other. A non-emotional example is the birth-oracle on Jacob and Esau as expressed in Rom. 9:12–13. An emotional equivalent of 'love-less-than' is in Gn. 29:31 with 30; and of either this or 'dislike' in Dt. 21:15–17.

Hebrew of verse 15a does not say 'there I *began to* hate them', as though God had taken a sudden and growing dislike to them at this place. Gilgal, for whatever reason, marked a climax rather than a beginning of these strained relations. If, as some think, the reference is to Israel's first clamour for a king – certainly a theme in Hosea: *e.g.* 13:9–11 – that confrontation in fact took place at Ramah (1 Sa. 8:4–9), not Gilgal (1 Sa. 11:12–15). So it seems more likely that the special sin of Gilgal lay in the flagrantly false worship – false by its immorality, hypocrisy and heresy (*cf.* 4:14–19) – which evidently flourished there even more than in its fellow sanctuaries at Bethel and elsewhere.

So the chapter ends with a reiteration of the nation's immediate prospect, which was equally God's sentence and their own choice; a fourfold doom of barrenness, carnage, estrangement and homelessness. The last of these, 'they shall be wanderers among the nations', was to become, tragically, part of their distinctive and proverbial reputation – yet it was not the last word that God would have for them. For this, see Romans 11 in its entirety, but especially verses 11–16 and 25 to the end.

Hosea 10:1–15
'Time to seek the Lord'

There is great variety in this chapter, for all its insistence on a single theme of warning. It draws now on early history (9), now on more recent memories (14); it bombards us with lively metaphors (4, 7, 11), ominous predictions (7–8), common-sense logic (13), snatches of current talk (3); it is always changing its angle of attack. But its thrust is positive: to spur the reader, not to stun him. The one gleam of light, the invitation of verse 12, is the *raison d'être* of the whole chapter.

Bounty and betrayal

10:1 *Israel is a luxuriant vine*
          that yields its fruit.
     The more his fruit increased
          the more altars he built;
     as his country improved
          he improved his pillars.

> 2 *Their heart is false;*
> *now they must bear their guilt.*
> *The Lord will break down their altars,*
> *and destroy their pillars.*

When Jesus said 'I am the true vine',[1] the vine of Israel was the background to His words – this favoured and once flourishing but ever disappointing specimen, whose promise and purpose He alone was fit to fulfil. As for Israel (and as for us, the True Vine's branches?), the more God did for them the more they misapplied it. Isaiah 5:1–7 follows the metaphor through, to speak of Israel's 'wild grapes' of violence and injustice; and Hosea did much the same in the previous chapter (9:10ff.), with his picture of their forebears as fruit that had rapidly gone rotten.

Now he uses it more freely, passing on to the literal fruitfulness of their land – God's gift – and the offensive crop of altars and pillars – man's wrong-headed response – that kept pace with this prosperity. Chapter 2 has already given us the clue to God's anger at this, for these were not only a material instead of a spiritual response: they were the paraphernalia of Baal worship, thinly disguised as worship of the Lord; and their prime object was to insure against lean times. As J. L. Mays has caustically remarked, 'the development of cultic sanctuaries was simply turning part of the profit back into the business. Altars and pillars were the holy machinery which produced the prosperity – a typically Canaanite understanding of cult.'[2]

Typically Canaanite, to be sure; and we may add, for our own instruction, typically carnal, not only in its calculating attitude to God but in its obsession with externals and its quickness to absorb the spirit of the surrounding culture. 'The more God did for them' (we might say about our own ecclesiastical record), 'the more structures they set up and the more they merged with their environment.'

Disenchantment

> 10:3 *For now they will say:*
> *'We have no king,*

[1] Jn. 15:1ff.　　[2] Mays, p. 139.

for we fear not the Lord,
   and a king, what could he do for us?'
4 They utter mere words;
   with empty oaths they make covenants;
so judgment springs up like poisonous weeds
   in the furrows of the field.
5 The inhabitants of Samaria tremble
   for the calf of Beth-aven.
Its people shall mourn for it,
   and its idolatrous priests shall wail over it,
   over its glory which has departed from it.
6 Yea, the thing itself shall be carried to Assyria,
   as tribute to the great king.
Ephraim shall be put to shame,
   and Israel shall be ashamed of his idol.

We might well wonder whether arrogance or apathy is the greater of two evils for a nation. For Israel, the mood had swung between the two, marked by their changing attitudes towards the throne: at one moment pinning all their hopes to kingship ('Give me a king and princes', 13:10), at another cheapening it with debauchery and tearing it apart with assassinations (7:3–7); finally, here in verse 3, shrugging it off as meaningless, along with everything else, from the Lord downwards. Only their superstition, their talisman the golden calf, will awaken any sense of loss by its removal.

When heaven is considered empty ('we fear not the Lord', 3), words and promises soon follow suit, and justice, so-called, becomes a parody of its true self – no longer towering impartially above the strong and the weak, but earthbound and tortuous, springing from the thoughts and policies of the moment; no longer a force for good and for the nation's health, but a source of poison. The picture of it as a weed which takes over a farmer's field (4) provides a startling contrast to the majestic metaphors of height and depth and clarity associated with true, divine justice ('on high, out of ... sight', Ps. 10:5; 'like the great deep', Ps. 36:6; 'as the light', Ho. 6:5).[3] The

---

[3] I understand 'judgment' here (4) in the prevailing OT sense of the 'justice' (cf. GNB) dispensed by a judge or practised as morality between one person and another. But it may have here its further meaning of punishment, or again (as in NEB; cf. NIV), litigation.

accusation is borne out by history. At best, humanism takes its estimate of morality and justice from ground level – from whatever happens to be a society's current mood and practice; while at worst, tyrants and demagogues equate it simply with their policies and interests. So the false morality strengthens its hold on the community, choking the true values as a wild crop smothers the good growth under its spreading carpet.

It is hardly surprising that the paragraph ends by predicting a typically confused human state of mind in verses 5 and 6: a sense of vanished glory, appropriately enough, yet attached to the very thing that was the nation's shame, the calf of Bethel.[4] In Samuel's day (as we saw in chapter 9 with the comments on verse 11) the captured ark of God had been lamented, as well it might be; but now Israel's tears will be for a captured idol and symbol of apostasy – for Jeroboam I had set it up at Bethel to create a rival cult against Jerusalem (1 Ki. 12:26–33). This is the mourning that springs from disappointment and wounded pride rather than repentance; a 'worldly grief' that leads no-where, rather than the godly grief that 'leads to salvation and brings no regret' (cf. 2 Cor. 7:10).

As a postscript to the passage, notice the expression 'the great king' (6), which has already met us at 5:13. Such was a title of the Assyrian monarchs; but the Hebrew text gives it a scornful twist, to read 'king Jareb' (AV, RV), 'a king who finds fault' (cf. RSV margin). George Adam Smith found the perfect equivalent: 'King Pick-Quarrel'.[5] In a single word Hosea has shown up the hopelessness of attempting to buy off so inveterate an aggressor.

Days of reckoning

10:7 *Samaria's king shall perish,*
like a chip on the face of the waters.
8 *The high places of Aven, the sin of Israel,*
shall be destroyed.
Thorn and thistle shall grow up
on their altars;

---

[4] Once again, as in 4:15, Bethel ('house of God') is renamed Beth-aven, 'house of iniquity'. *Cf.* verse 8, where it is simply 'Aven'.
[5] Smith, pp. 263, 287.

> *and they shall say to the mountains, Cover us,*
> *and to the hills, Fall upon us.*

> 9 *From the days of Gibeah, you have sinned, O Israel;*
> *there they have continued.*
> *Shall not war overtake them in Gibeah?*
> 10 *I will come against the wayward people to chastise them;*
> *and nations shall be gathered against them*
> *when they are chastised for their double iniquity.*

There is never a lack of lively imagery in this book. Here, in the space of the first two verses, three very different pictures put a rapid end to thoughts of human self-sufficiency. The king, 'of whom we said, "Under his shadow we shall live among the nations"',[6] would prove to be no massive oak, deep-rooted and reassuring, but a twig on the surface of a torrent, overtaken by events and whisked helplessly away. If that picture is all turbulence, the next one, of shrines and altars deserted and overgrown, is ominously still. Added to this, the nickname 'Aven' ('iniquity') for these holy places, and the comment that they are 'the sin of Israel', together say the last word on man-made religion. But the last word on human arrogance and independence is reserved for the end of the verse: 'they shall say to the mountains, Cover us . . .' – a cry which the New Testament will take up twice: first to predict the still greater horrors awaiting the Jerusalem of AD 70 as the logical outcome of its Good Friday choice, and secondly to portray the terrors of the Last Judgment, with men of every rank and nation 'calling to the mountains and rocks, "Fall on us and hide us from the face of him who is seated on the throne, and from the wrath of the Lamb"' (Lk. 23:30; Rev. 6:16).

So we are not left to contemplate the downfall of Samaria[7] on its own, safely isolated in the eighth century BC. It meets us as a foretaste of still weightier events, as indeed are all the local, limited tragedies of history. Our Lord laid down for us the right and wrong reactions to such happenings, when He was asked to comment on a massacre:

[6] *Cf.* La. 4:20. Although these words refer to the Davidic king of Judah, they express something of the exalted view of kingship that was current at the time, as 13:10 implies.

[7] See the map on p. 129 and the diagram on pp. 134f.

'Do you think that these Galileans were worse sinners than all the other Galileans, because they suffered thus? I tell you, No; but unless you repent you will all likewise perish. Or those eighteen upon whom the tower in Siloam fell and killed them, do you think that they were worse offenders than all the others who dwelt in Jerusalem? I tell you, No; but unless you repent you will all likewise perish' (Lk. 13:2–5).

We can hardly complain that the last act of our human drama has been under-rehearsed!

Once more, as so often in these closing chapters, God now reinforces what He has to say with a reminder of past history. The name Gibeah (9) is doubly potent, linking Hosea's generation with the most vicious episode in Israel's past (see the comments on 9:9, p. 87) and with its aftermath, the destructive civil war of Judges 20. But verse 10 appoints foreign nations, not fellow-Israelites this time, as the means of punishment. The fulfilment is recorded in 2 Kings 17:6 and, for good measure, 24–41.

Before we pass on from verse 10, two details may be worth pointing out. First, the opening line in the Hebrew text reads simply, 'At my desire (i.e., when I so decide) I will chastise them.'[8] Secondly, the last line reads 'to bind them to their two sins'. If this is right (but 'bind' could be a copying error for the similar word 'chastise'), it makes two points about the judgment that must fall: first, that it awaits God's chosen time, and secondly that it ties the sinner to the sinner's choice. Nothing could be less fortuitous or less arbitrary.

As for the 'double iniquity', many suggested meanings have been offered. Among the most likely is that it refers to Israel's resort to Baal in its worship and to worldly allies in its politics – both of which are major accusations in these chapters. Another is that the allusion is to their rejection first of God as their true king and then of David as His anointed. This double defection is implied in 3:5, but that passage is hardly close at hand here. Further suggestions fasten on the reference to Gibeah just before this, and see the two sins either as those of Israel's past and present, or else as the outrage of Judges 19 plus the dis-

---

[8] RSV's longer first line, 'I will come against the wayward people to chastise them', is an adaptation of the LXX of verses 9b – 10a.

obedient reign of Saul (who made Gibeah his centre). Some of these interpretations seem over-subtle, and it may be that the simplest of all should be followed: that like the 'three transgressions ... and ... four' of Amos 1:3, 6, *etc.*, the two iniquities mean just the repeated or persistent acts of Israel's disobedience.

A choice of harvests

10:11 *Ephraim was a trained heifer*
that loved to thresh,
and I spared her fair neck;
but I will put Ephraim to the yoke,
Judah must plough,
Jacob must harrow for himself.
12 *Sow for yourselves righteousness,*
reap the fruit of steadfast love;
break up your fallow ground,
for it is the time to seek the Lord,
that he may come and rain salvation upon you.

13 *You have ploughed iniquity,*
you have reaped injustice,
you have eaten the fruit of lies.
Because you have trusted in your chariots
and in the multitude of your warriors,
14 *therefore the tumult of war shall arise among your people,*
and all your fortresses shall be destroyed,
as Shalman destroyed Beth-arbel on the day of battle;
mothers were dashed in pieces with their children.
15 *Thus it shall be done to you, O house of Israel,*
because of your great wickedness.
In the storm the king of Israel
shall be utterly cut off.

This is very typical of Hosea's preaching, with its glance back to a happier past (11a), its resourceful use of metaphors – here drawn from farming – and its conclusion in unmistakably plain speaking.

The point about the heifer in the opening verse (11) is that threshing was a comparatively light task, made pleasant by the fact that the creature was unmuzzled and free to eat (Dt. 25:4) as it pulled the threshing-sledge over the gathered corn. This owner's pride in his beast, and his consideration for it (*cf.* Pr. 12:10), together with the creature's obedience and content-ment, provides one of the many affectionate touches in these troubled chapters. There will be another with the same imagery of man and beast in 11:4.

But the idyllic scene had to change. Perhaps we are meant to see that in any case there must be a transition to hard and testing work, in any worth-while enterprise and for any growth to maturity:

'Although he was a Son, he learned obedience through what he suffered'. 'For the Lord disciplines him whom he loves' (Heb. 5:8; 12:6).

But in Israel's case (and Judah's, 11b) the hardship was com-pounded by her retreat into obstinacy. 'Like a stubborn heifer, Israel is stubborn' (4:16). So the yoke of verse 11 would no longer be the well-fitting one of God's ideal design, but the harsh, heavy collar of slavery. What would be said one day of Babylon and Judah would be doubly true of Assyria and Ephraim:

'I gave them into your hand,
    you showed them no mercy;
on the aged you made your yoke
    exceedingly heavy'   (Is. 47:6).

Yet the picture is not one of unrelieved or pointless gloom. The yoke, after all, is there to serve the best of ends, the harvest, through the best of means, the plough and harrow. So verse 12a is as positive as it is practical, and 12b as generous as it is urgent. The expression 'fallow ground' was extraordinarily well suited to describe a people doubly impervious to the good seed of God's word, both by the tangled growth of worldly notions and preoccupations which had taken hold of them, and by the hard crust beneath it all, of wills and attitudes never broken into penitence.

A later prophet was to take this up and spell it out with the call, 'Break up your fallow ground, and sow not among thorns' (Je. 4:3); and still the parable of the Sower (Mt. 13) speaks to such a situation, forbidding us to confine Hosea's challenge simply to his own generation. As for his urgent conclusion, '... it is the time to seek the Lord ...', certainly we can see with hindsight just how little time was left for Israel, whose kingdom fell almost before Hosea had finished speaking. But again it is a warning that speaks today – indeed, as Hebrews 3:13 puts it, 'every day, as long as it is called "today"' – since the present is the only time that lies to hand, with the past beyond recall and the future beyond conjecture.

With verse 13 the warning note returns, to mount to a new climax. First it takes up the metaphors of the plough, the harvest and the table, this time to highlight the iron chain of causality between them. In verse 12 it was a golden chain, leading to 'the fruit of steadfast love'[9] as surely as this one leads to 'the fruit of lies' (13). What such fruit consists of – in a word, the breakdown of all sound relationships and the corrupting of all values – is pictured poetically in the 'grapes of poison' of Deuteronomy 32:32, and expounded in unsparing detail in Isaiah 59:1–15. For another and more famous saying of Hosea on sowing and reaping, see 8:7 and the comment there (p. 79).

But the metaphors now give way to stark, literal reality; and the charge of injustice and treachery is supplemented by that of military jingoism as the chapter ends. It hardly matters that we can only guess at the identities of Shalman and Beth-arbel,[10] for we can gather what those names meant to Hosea's first hearers: names as horrific to them as 'Hitler' or 'Belsen' to us. Yet, to make it worse, a conqueror's atrocities against mothers and children (14b) were clearly all too common,[11] even if an extra ruthlessness or the force of an event fresh in the memory added

[9] The LXX reads 'the fruit of' (Heb. $p^e r\hat{\imath}$) in verse 12, matching the expression of verse 13. The Massoretic text, however, has 'according to' ($l^e p\hat{\imath}$) in verse 12.

[10] Shalman is most probably short for Shalmaneser of Assyria: either Shalmaneser V (727–722 BC), whose march to besiege Samaria could well have taken him through Beth-arbel (? the Arbela of 1 Macc. 9:2, near the west shore of the lake of Galilee); or alternatively Shalmaneser III of the previous century (859–824 BC), who campaigned against Syria, Hauran and Israel in 841 BC, and whose route could well have included this Arbela or another Arbela near Pella, east of the Jordan. See M. Astour, 'The First Assyrian Invasion of Israel', *JAOS* 91 (1971), pp. 386f., for the latter view; but more cautiously M. Elat in *IEJ* 25 (1975), p. 31, note 25.

[11] See 2 Ki. 8:12; 15:16; Ps. 137:8f.; Is. 13:16; Am. 1:13; Na. 3:10.

a special sharpness to the present warning. Any romantic eagerness we may feel towards military or revolutionary adventures should be chilled by our contemplating the sequence of *'Because ... therefore'* in 13b, 14a, and of *'as ... thus'* in 14b, 15a.

There is no need to 'correct' the final sentence so as to open with the words 'In the storm' (RSV, JB).[12] The existing text, 'At daybreak', makes perfectly good sense, whether rendered in NIV as 'When that day dawns' or, more freely, 'As sure as day dawns' (NEB). It shows that the king can no more postpone the day of reckoning than he could stem the torrent of verse 7 that was to sweep him away.

Hosea 11:1–11
'How can I give you up?'

This chapter is one of the boldest in the Old Testament – indeed in the whole Bible – in exposing to us the mind and heart of God in human terms. We are always in danger of thinking of divine majesty in terms which we have learnt from earthly potentates, 'the kings of the Gentiles' whom our Lord summed up in Luke 22:25–27 in contrast to Himself. Even when we speak of God as Father we may hesitate in case we read too much into the word. But our chief danger is in reading too little from it, drawing our ideas either from an earthly father's indulgence, caring too little for his children's training, or from his self-indulgence, taking the convenient path of a domestic tyrant.

Here, by contrast, we are made to see this title in terms of accepted cost and anguish. God as a father rebuffed, torn between agonizing alternatives, may seem too human altogether; but this is the price of bringing home to us the fact that divine love is more, not less, ardent and vulnerable than ours. 'For' (as verse 9 will remind us, correcting our inverted values) 'I am God and not man.' Once more, as in chapter 3, it is He, not we, who sets the pace and who stays the course against every discouragement and provocation that ingratitude can offer.

---

[12] *I.e.*, to substitute a conjectured *śaʿar*, 'storm', for *šaḥar*, 'dawn'.

The cold shoulder

11:1 When Israel was a child, I loved him,
    and out of Egypt I called my son.
 2 The more I called them,
    the more they went from me;
  they kept sacrificing to the Baals,
    and burning incense to idols.

 3 Yet it was I who taught Ephraim to walk,
    I took them up in my arms;
  but they did not know that I healed them.
 4 I led them with cords of compassion,
    with the bands of love,
  and I became to them as one
    who eases the yoke on their jaws,
    and I bent down to them and fed them.

More than once we have been reminded of the bright promise of Israel's youth, so rapidly to fade.[1] The promise arose out of God's grace rather than their good qualities, and the fading of it out of their sheer perversity – for it is one of Hosea's emphases that Israel's sin, so far from springing from ignorance or hardship, was their reply to heaven's kindness and concern.

The grace of God shines out at once in the words 'I loved him' (implying, when used by God, not the involuntary emotional reaction which it tends to mean to us, but a choice as free as it is affectionate[2]), and still more clearly in His naming Israel 'my son'.

Incidentally the quotation of this verse in Matthew 2:15 is far from arbitrary. Israel in its childhood was already set apart for the world's ultimate blessing, and was described to Pharaoh as God's 'first-born son' (Ex. 4:22f.). By God's providence it had taken refuge in Egypt, but must return to its own land to fulfil its calling. Therefore, although it had been threatened with extinction through (among other things) the massacre of its infant sons, it was miraculously delivered. Not surprisingly the infant Christ, who summed up in His person all that Israel was

---

[1] See 6:4; 9:10; 10:1, 11; 13:1, 4–6.
[2] Note the *'not because ..., but ... because ...'* in Dt. 7:7–8, where God speaks more fully of this loving choice.

called to be, was likewise threatened and delivered; and although the details differed, the early pattern was re-enacted in its essentials, ending with God's Son restored to God's land to fulfil the task marked out for Him.

After that digression, the tragic anticlimax of verse 2 comes to us with added force. Between the great beginning and great fulfilment of the saying, 'I called my son', there stretches the long age in which the words 'I called'[3] received the worst of answers. There are similar sequences of 'The more ... the more', equally perverse, at 4:7 and 10:1, and it would be a mistake to imagine that this off-handed reaction to divine love and to prosperity was confined to ancient Israel. Familiarity can still breed contempt, and success conceit, as though the very gifts that bring prosperity were not gifts at all, and the patient love of God were weakness.

The tenderness of verses 3 and 4 completes two (or perhaps one – see below) of the pictures God has used in nearby passages. Fatherly love, merely stated in verse 1, is now charmingly portrayed in a scene that any family will recognize, with father absorbed in coaxing and supporting the child's first staggering steps; picking him up when he tires or tumbles; 'making the place better' when he hurts himself (though Isaiah 66:13 will remind us that father is only second-best at this). But Ephraim (that is, Israel) is a child no longer. Like some aloof and scornful adolescent he has forgotten or never realized – or simply does not want to know – what he owes to this relationship.

The second picture, that of verse 4, seems to take up and surpass that of 10:11a (the contented heifer and the considerate master). The heavenly farmer is now shown, in retrospect, as having treated his beast more as a pet than as a working animal.[4] Every detail of this pampering drives home the extraordinary graciousness that Israel has experienced, far beyond anything that she had any right to expect, or any prospect of receiving at the hands of her new masters. The next paragraph will make the last point brutally clear.

---

[3] 'The more I called . . .', etc., is the LXX reading, adopted (rightly, I think) by the modern versions. The MT, with 'The more they called . . .', etc., makes the same point but leaves the 'they' (presumably the prophets) unintroduced and unidentified.

[4] An attractive alternative is to read verse 4 as continuing the metaphor of

The cruel consequences

11:5 *They shall return to the land of Egypt,*
and Assyria shall be their king,
because they have refused to return to me.
6 *The sword shall rage against their cities,*
consume the bars of their gates,
and devour them in their fortresses.
7 *My people are bent on turning away from me;*
so they are appointed to the yoke,
and none shall remove it.

Ever since chapter 7, with its picture of Ephraim flitting between Egypt and Assyria like a flustered bird (7:11), every chapter has named one or both of these great powers as her obsession and her downfall. In the comment on 8:13 we saw something of the reproach and irony in the thought of a return to Egypt;⁵ and now the word 'return' is taken up and used most tellingly in both its senses, literal and spiritual. Nowhere is it plainer than here that the unseen movement of the soul in turning to God (5b) or turning away (7a) is the decisive one, to be followed by inevitable consequences in the realm that we call practical. The physical return to Egypt – as refugees! – was certain from the moment of their refusal of a spiritual return to God.

<hr>

father and child, as in NEB (*cf.* JB, GNB): '. . . that I harnessed them in leading-strings and led them with bonds of love – that I had lifted them like a little child to my cheek . . .'. But this requires emending *'ōl* (yoke) to *'ul* (baby, suckling), and *lᵉḥêhem* (their cheeks or jaws) to *leḥyî* or *lᵉḥāyāy* (my cheek(s)) – and attractiveness is too little reason to alter a text that already makes sense. Admittedly the text seems disturbed elsewhere in the chapter (see on verse 7); but each passage must be treated on its own merits.

⁵ As AV, RV indicate, the Heb. text has the word 'not' (*lō'*) before 'return'. But in view of the repeated predictions of such a return in 8:13; 9:3, 6; 11:11, NIV legitimately takes this as an implied question. 'Will they not return . . .?' (see the footnote to 4:16b, p. 56). An alternative is to follow LXX in reading this word as *lô* ('to him'), taken as the last word of verse 4 (*e.g.*, JB: 'stooping down to him I gave him *[lô]* his food'), not the first word of verse 5. Sounding alike, *lō'* and *lô* were easily confused by copyists: *cf.* the famous example in Is. 9:3a ('*not* increased the joy', AV, corrected by later translations to agree with 3b by reading *lô* rather than *lō'*). For a more subtle interpretation of our verse, distinguishing between a typical and a literal return to Egypt, see *The New Bible Commentary Revised* (IVP, 1970), *ad loc.*

Likewise the rejection of God as king has to end not merely with the disappearance of the kings they chose instead of Him (the theme of 10:3, 7, 15) but with the iron rule of a foreign super-power. If RSV is right in verse 7b (but it is rather a big 'if'), this 'yoke'[6] stands in marked contrast to the one that was handled so gently in verse 4; and on any reading of the text there is now held out no prospect of relief.

The warm resolve

11:8 *How can I give you up, O Ephraim!*
      How can I hand you over, O Israel!
   How can I make you like Admah!
      How can I treat you like Zeboiim!
   My heart recoils within me,
      my compassion grows warm and tender.
 9 *I will not execute my fierce anger,*
      I will not again destroy Ephraim;
 for I am God and not man,
      the Holy One in your midst,
      and I will not come to destroy.

Suddenly the fearful mechanisms of moral cause and political effect, of national guilt and judgment, of betrayal and estrangement, are interrupted by this passionate intervention, purely from disinterested love. No matter that the Lord may now seem wholly swayed by impulse and emotion: we are nearer a true knowledge of Him in such terms than in the bloodless definitions of theological philosophy. Elsewhere Scripture takes ample care of what such definitions seek to safeguard, but it never takes the warmth out of love, the fire out of anger or the audacity out of grace.

So the very thought of abandoning the people He has lived amongst ('in your midst', 9), to an extinction like that of the

---

6 The Heb. text reads 'and (though) they call (upon) him to the height' (*'el-'al* – see footnote on 7:16), which NEB renders as 'though they call on their high god', while AV, NIV interpret 'the height' (*'al*) as 'the Most High'. JB, however, treats *'al* as a miscopying of *ba'al* (Baal), and RSV revocalizes it as *'ōl*, 'yoke' (see the previous footnote), and modifies the form and meaning of the verb 'to call', to yield the sentence, 'they are appointed to the yoke'. This makes a striking companion to 10:11 and 11:4, but is excessively conjectural.

cities of the plain,[7] stirs God to strong revulsion. But how does this fit in with what in fact transpired? For Ephraim/Israel (the northern kingdom) fell in 722 BC and was deported to Assyria. One answer could be that she was given, after this prophecy, yet another chance to repent. More probably the answer lies in the remnant who threw in their lot with Judah, and whose descendants returned with them from Babylon (1 Ch. 9:1–3) to be part of the continuing Israel which meets us in the New Testament as the parent stock of the church.[8] The next paragraph seems to bear this out.

The great homecoming

11:10 *They shall go after the Lord,*
he will roar like a lion;
yea, he will roar,
and his sons shall come trembling from the west;
11 *they shall come trembling like birds from Egypt,*
and like doves from the land of Assyria;
and I will return them to their homes, says the Lord.

God's mercy, in the great soliloquy of verses 8 and 9, decreed survival and a future for His people, when they deserved neither. But (as the rest of the book has shown) nothing facile would do, for without a change of heart survival would mean only a repetition of the past. So it is a chastened people, 'trembling ... trembling', that will at last come home from being 'wanderers among the nations' (9:17). The 'silly dove' of 7:11, always flitting between Egypt and Assyria, will have had its fill of both, and of the lands beyond the sea, and be thankful for its own nest. More important, it will be the Lord whom Israel will 'go after' (10), not the 'lovers' whom she had once pursued (2:5).

All this is seen as happening only at His signal, the lion's roar with which He leaps into action – for the Bible consistently portrays the Day of the Lord as one of terror, by its judgment

---

[7] Admah and Zeboiim were destroyed with Sodom and Gomorrah. Dt. 29:23 recalls this, in a passage which threatens Israel with just such a fate as theirs.
[8] See Romans 11, throughout.

on a wicked world, though also of delight by its ending of that evil.[9]

It is not easy to know what stage of history is in mind here: whether some intermediate day of the lion's roar, such as the overthrow of Babylon which brought a remnant of Israel (including some from these northern tribes) home to Jerusalem;[10] or the spiritual homecoming of God's 'sons' (10b) of many nations in the gospel age (in line with Paul's quotation of Ho. 2:23 and 1:10, in Rom. 9:25–26); or again the great turning of Israel to the Lord which is predicted in Romans 11:12, 25ff. What is certain is that the final event will far surpass our wisest thoughts and wildest expectations.

Hosea 11:12[1] – 12:14
Look back and learn!

If we have any misgivings over treating the early stories of the Bible as texts for today, this chapter should dispel them. It reads almost as sermon notes on the life of Jacob and on the exodus from Egypt; and Hosea has already drawn on other potent incidents of the past as mirrors of the present and pointers to the future.[2]

But first he is severely topical, assessing Ephraim and Judah as they are in his own day.

My Lord Time-server and my Lord Turn-about

The following translation is that of the New International Version (NIV), adopted here for reasons which will appear below.

11:12 *Ephraim has surrounded me with lies,*
the house of Israel with deceit.

---

[9] While in Amos the lion's roar (Am. 1:2) announces an imminent series of local judgments, Je. 25:30–38 presents it on a world-wide scale, and Joel 3:16 as enough to shake the universe. 'But', adds Joel, 'the Lord is a refuge to his people.'

[10] See again 1 Ch. 9:1–3.

[1] In the Heb. Bible the new chapter begins at this earlier point, with good reason.

[2] *E.g.* 6:7 (?); 9:9; 10:9f.; 11:1f.; *cf.* 13:10f.

And Judah is unruly against God,
  even against the faithful Holy One.
12:1 *Ephraim feeds on the wind;*
  he pursues the east wind all day
  and multiplies lies and violence.
He makes a treaty with Assyria
  and sends olive oil to Egypt.
2 *The Lord has a charge to bring against Judah;*
  he will punish Jacob according to his ways
  and repay him according to his deeds.

The heading we have given to this paragraph calls for two comments. First, the fanciful names come (as most readers will recognize) from *The Pilgrim's Progress*, where they sum up two leading citizens of the town of Fair-speech. But secondly, whereas Judah, to judge by the NIV text printed here, deserves the second of these names, some translations would present him in a very different light. For example, RSV:

  'but Judah is still known by God,
    and is faithful to the Holy One.'

There are, however, two objections to RSV's favourable picture. First, in the next breath God brings 'an indictment against Judah' (2, RSV); and secondly, the statement that Judah is still 'known by' God and faithful to Him is based on the Septuagint, not the Hebrew text. The Hebrew says that Judah still 'plays fast and loose' with God.[3] The second line of that couplet must take this into account, as in, *e.g.*, NIV or NEB.[4]

So both kingdoms are rebuked, but chiefly Ephraim which is Hosea's mission field. One lesson that emerges from this pair of verses is that double-talk, whatever it does to the listener, certainly corrupts the talker. The religious 'lies' and 'deceit' of 11:12 are linked by more than chance with the inner emptiness

---

[3] The Heb. *rād* is from the root *rwd*, the verb used in Je. 2:31 to express playing truant, running wild ('we have broken away', NEB; 'we are free', RSV). And AV, RV had to emend *rād* to *rādâ* to arrive at their translation, 'ruleth'.

[4] NIV ('even against the faithful Holy One') sounds a little forced, but *cf.* GNB, RV mg. Alternatively NEB may be right in interpreting the plural word *qᵉdōšîm* not as 'the Holy One', but in its more obvious sense as 'holy ones'; hence, freely, 'still loyal to the idols he counts holy'.

and futile aims of 12:1a (another of Hosea's caustic little sketches) and with the double-dealing of 12:1b – for each reacts on the other. It happened this way in Hosea's time, in a downward spiral of meaningless religion (4:6; 7:14; 8:11ff.), moral anarchy (*e.g.* 4:1ff.), feverish hedonism (4:10ff.), perfidy in politics and diplomacy (7:6f., 11), and in the end, friendlessness (8:8–10) and ruin. It would not be hard to find at least parts of this pattern reproduced wherever other groups and nations have started on such a path.

Yet while the chapter takes us through some of these stages, it also braces us with reminders of what can happen when God and man take hold of one another and when God's day of liberation dawns. So we turn our minds to a founding father and a formative event: to Jacob and to the exodus.

Wrestling Jacob

12:3 *In the womb he took his brother by the heel,*
and in his manhood he strove with God.
4 *He strove with the angel and prevailed,*
he wept and sought his favour.
He met God at Bethel,
and there God spoke with him –
5 *the Lord the God of hosts,*
the Lord is his name:
6 '*So you, by the help of your God, return,*
hold fast to love and justice,
and wait continually for your God.'

In only a stroke or two the first couplet brings the whole of Jacob's story into focus by means of his two names, Jacob and Israel. The glimpse of him, born with his hand clutching Esau's heel (Gn. 25:26), gave him his birth-name ('he-is-at-the-heel'[5]); and for years his dealings with his fellows were to confirm all that was sinister in the name, as of one who steals up from behind to outwit and overreach you. Esau, who was bargained out of his birthright and tricked out of his blessing,

---

[5] Normally the name, which is found elsewhere in the ancient world, would mean 'May He (God) be at your heels', *i.e.*, be your rearguard. But, like the name Isaac ('May He smile' [upon you]), it had a double meaning within the family, commemorating a very special moment.

cried, 'Is he not rightly named Jacob? For he has supplanted me ("Jacobed me") these two times . . .' (Gn. 27:36). Even Laban, that master of manoeuvre, found he had met his match in this man.

His ultimate name, Israel, speaks very differently: of tenacity without stealth ('he strives'), and of a preoccupation, in the last resort, not with man but with God.[6] The transformation that this implies is put with beautiful economy in the first two lines of verse 4, initially portraying his aggression and will to win, redirected now towards the nobler end of having power with God (yet still in terms of imposing his own will on his great adversary), but finally portraying him as a suppliant for grace; his arrogance broken, but not his eagerness. The story is told in Genesis 32:22–32.

Even so, verse 4 has one more point to make: that the re-making of the man had its origin not in his own enterprise, but in God's initiative revealed at Bethel long before,[7] in that classic display of grace unexpected, unsought and overwhelming.

Hosea is about to drive the lesson home with the great appeal of verse 6: 'So *you* . . .' But before he does so he reiterates the name of God, dwelling on it in verse 5 with special emphasis. If we wonder why he pauses at this point, we may notice that, for once, he has called the chief shrine of northern Israel by its right name, Bethel, 'house of God', instead of by its savage nickname Beth-aven, 'house of wickedness'. For it was *God* whom Jacob had met there: God, not a golden calf (10:5; 13:2); and if Israel would learn from Jacob, this was the first lesson it must face.

Now, in verse 6, the heartfelt challenge can be made: '*So you . . . return*' – for your name is not Jacob/Israel for nothing! If you are more 'Jacob' than 'Israel', so was he when the call came, in the far country, with the words, 'Return to the land of your fathers . . . and I will be with you.'[8] And if he received his new name when he insisted 'I will not let you go, unless you bless me', so you are to be equally in earnest: to 'hold fast' to His will, and 'wait continually' for His presence. (This is all the

[6] Israel appears to mean basically 'May God strive (for him)', but the wrestling context gave it the force of 'He strives with God' (Gn. 32:28).

[7] Gn. 28:10–22.

[8] Gn. 31:3; cf. 35:1, '. . . to Bethel, . . . to the God who appeared to you when you fled from your brother Esau.'

more pointed on account of its background in 6:1–6, where Israel's love was 'like the dew that goes early away'.)

If this seems too high a challenge, we overlook Hosea's nuance in phrasing it not simply as 'Return to', but rather, 'You will return with' – *i.e.*, with the help of[9] – 'your God'. Nothing is then impossible.

Affluent Ephraim

12:7 *A trader, in whose hands are false balances,*
    he loves to oppress.
  8 *Ephraim has said, 'Ah, but I am rich,*
    I have gained wealth for myself';
    but all his riches can never offset
    the guilt he has incurred.
  9 *I am the Lord your God*
    from the land of Egypt;
    I will again make you dwell in tents,
    as in the days of the appointed feast.

Anticlimax! Ephraim's is no wistful refusal like the rich young ruler's, but brazen, Laodicean[10] – and worse still, Canaanite. For 'Canaan' is the word translated here 'A trader', branding Ephraim a true successor to the old corrupt inhabitants of the land. In cold print, his bland assurance that his extorted riches carry no guilt – or none to speak of[11] – and even put him above the law, is patently absurd. Yet human attitudes, which venerate success and, at a safe distance, admire a clever rogue, still help to build up this cocksureness in the man who sells his soul to the present.

To this, God's answer is another flashback to the past – this time not Jacob but the exodus. He makes His point first from the opening salvo of the Ten Commandments, 'I am the Lord your God [who brought you up] from the land of Egypt' – words as familiar to them as the Lord's Prayer to us – and then

---

[9] So RSV, NEB; *cf.* this Heb. preposition in, *e.g.*, 1:7, 'I will deliver them "by" the Lord . . . not "by" bow nor "by" sword,' *etc.*; likewise the well-known Zc. 4:6. Alternatively it may imply 'return (and rest) *in* thy God' (so BDB, p. 88b).

[10] *Cf.* Rev. 3:17.

[11] The Hebrew of 8b (9b, Heb.) is most accurately rendered in RV: '. . . they shall find in me none iniquity that were sin.'

from the ritual of the pilgrim feast of tabernacles.

It is a double thrust. First (in effect): 'Was it for *this* that I redeemed you? To make you a bunch of Canaanites?' And secondly: 'When you re-live the exodus each year, camping out as your fathers did, is it only make-believe? Or is it to re-learn the lesson of those days, that man does not live by bread alone?'

So, if they will only take it, there is healing and not mere doom in God's resolve to strip away the comforts that have turned these pilgrims into profiteers. The apparent threat, 'I will again make you dwell in tents' (9), is of a piece with what was said in 2:14f.,

> Therefore, behold, I will allure her,
>> and bring her into the wilderness,
>> and speak tenderly to her . . .
> And there she shall answer me as in the days of her youth,
>> as at the time when she came out of the land of Egypt.

This is the spirit of the whole book. But just because it seeks a free response, it may be met with obdurate refusal; and there is no attempt to hide that possibility or to mask its fatal consequences.

Prophets without honour

12:10 *I spoke to the prophets;*
> *it was I who multiplied visions,*
> *and through the prophets gave parable..*
11 *If there is iniquity in Gilead*
> *they shall surely come to naught;*
> *if in Gilgal they sacrifice bulls,*
> *their altars also shall be like stone heaps*
> *on the furrows of the field.*
12 *(Jacob fled to the land of Aram,*
> *there Israel did service for a wife,*
> *and for a wife he herded sheep.)*
13 *By a prophet the Lord brought Israel up from Egypt,*
> *and by a prophet he was preserved.*
14 *Ephraim has given bitter provocation;*
> *so his Lord will leave his bloodguilt upon him,*
> *and will turn back upon him his reproaches.*

The close of the chapter has the broken, disjointed sound of agitation and distress. But the way verse 13 reverts to the opening theme (10), the role of *the prophets*, suggests that here at least there is a unifying thread, a central emphasis. It is that God's dealings with man have always been directed to the mind and conscience, which are the prophets' great concern; and the nation will be judged on that high plane alone.

The opening verse (10) goes out of its way to stress the fact that God, not man, is the fount and origin of prophecy (*'it was I . . .'*) and of its strange and varied ways of speaking. 'The prophet is a fool,' people were saying; 'the man of the spirit is mad' (9:7); but the prophet's visions and parables were not mere eccentricities: they were the word of God. This at once raises the question (for us as much as for the ancient Israelites) why God, who could speak with the precision of a lawgiver and the persuasive clarity of a wisdom teacher, should also dazzle us with visions and tease us with parables. The answer, at least in part, is that the prophet was sent to make men *think*, and to confront them with the signs of their own time and with the living God, who is not shut away timelessly behind His laws and liturgies, but turns upon us 'the eyes of his glory' (as Isaiah puts it: Is. 3:8, RV) and brings whole nations into judgment.

So – and here is the connection between verses 10 and 11 – God names actual places, far and near, that are ripening for judgment, and pours fine scorn on pious superstitions, punning on the falsely venerated Gilgal with the disrespectful plural of *gal*, 'a rubble heap'. This divine impatience with religiosity burned fiercely in the prophets, especially in Hosea's great contemporaries, Amos, Micah and Isaiah, but supremely in our Lord, whose sustained invective in Matthew 23 surpasses even that of the Old Testament for both brilliance of expression and depth of concern.

Passing over verse 12 for the moment,[12] verse 13's repetition, *'By a prophet . . ., by a prophet'*, makes a more important point than may appear at first sight. It is not simply that the prophets can trace their spiritual lineage back to Moses, though this is true.[13] Rather, it insists that the exodus was above all a spiritual event, not just a liberation movement. Moses' greatness was

[12] See the Additional Note on p. 113.
[13] See Dt. 18:15–22, which foresees a line of prophets between Moses and the ultimate prophet, Christ (*cf.* Acts 3:22ff.).

not that he stood up to Pharaoh, but that he stood before God and knew Him face to face. Mount Sinai, first with the revelation at the burning bush, and subsequently with the giving of the Law and Covenant, gave the whole enterprise its point. It was no mere detour, no formal church parade on the march to victory. 'I bore you on eagles' wings and brought you *to myself*.'[14] Here, in knowing God, was Israel's *raison d'être* and true stability: 'by a prophet he was preserved' – for 'where there is no prophecy the people cast off restraint'.[15]

It is still more fatal, as the final verse makes clear, to have prophecy and no use for it. That was Ephraim's 'bitter provocation'. It is the special danger of a once-enlightened nation, church or individual, whose appetite for truth has failed for lack of exercise in what St John would call '*doing* truth' (*cf.* Jn. 3:21, AV).

Additional Note on Hosea 12:12

Verse 12 seems to be a parenthesis, supplying the missing part of the patriarch's life-story as summarized in verse 3, where it was perhaps excluded so as to leave the Jacob-Israel contrast all the clearer. But its present place may have a subtler purpose. J. L. Mays draws attention to the repetition of the Hebrew root for 'kept' (RSV 'herded … preserved') in verses 12 and 13 (13–14, Heb.), and sees in this an implied contrast between the human shepherd, so limited in scope, and the divine one – for it could well be that Israel found its pride and reassurance too much in its former ancestor, too little in the living God of the exodus and the prophets. That ancestor is therefore portrayed now in the soberest of colours: a fugitive rather than a pilgrim, a keeper of sheep rather than the shepherd of a nation; his motivation, for years, totally domestic. Hero-worship, we are gently reminded, is seldom even true to the past, let alone valid for the present.

Hosea 13:1–16
The unmaking of a kingdom

This is the climax of Hosea's prophecies of doom, but not

---

[14] Ex. 19:4, spoken at Mount Sinai. *Cf.* Ex. 3:12, 18.
[15] Pr. 29:18.

the climax of the book. That distinction is reserved (apart from one remarkable verse here) for the next chapter, the great vision of renewal; but both were due to be fulfilled. The northern kingdom, as we have already seen, was due to fall in 722 BC, never to reappear; but the New Testament already celebrates the greater things that were to lie beyond this tragedy.

The one dazzling exception (as I see it) to the darkness of this chapter is the great taunt of verse 14 against the Last Enemy. Most modern translations, unhappily, turn this upside-down, in the supposed interests of consistency; therefore at that point I have substituted the more literal rendering of the NIV for that of the RSV (as I have also done in one other place, 11:12ff.), defending the decision in the comments on that verse.

Vanished dignity

13:1 *When Ephraim spoke, men trembled;*
he was exalted in Israel;
but he incurred guilt through Baal and died.
2 *And now they sin more and more,*
and make for themselves molten images,
idols skilfully made of their silver,
all of them the work of craftsmen.
Sacrifice to these, they say.
Men kiss calves!
3 *Therefore they shall be like the morning mist*
or like the dew that goes early away,
like the chaff that swirls from the threshing floor
or like smoke from a window.

If there is one fact about human fortunes which history almost dins into us, it is their instability; and historians can show any number of economic, political and other reasons for the changes that turn the giants of one era into the weaklings of the next. Here, not the power-changes abroad nor the factions at home are blamed for the sad state of Ephraim, but a much earlier and subtler shift within the mind: from the Lord to Baal. At that point Ephraim 'died', as surely as Adam did, although like Adam he went on living, to all outward appearance. To make it still more imperceptible, this fickleness had posed as only a broadening of the way in which one served the Lord, as the comments on chapter 2 have shown. But such pluralism ignored the very first commandment (pointedly alluded to in verse 4 and previously in 12:9), and led straight on, by its veneration of idols, to the breaking of the second. There is a powerful jolt administered in verse 2 by the sudden change of focus, from the spectacle of skilful craftsmen and precious metals to that of the religious idiocy they served. The end of the expensive exercise, one which employed the talents of God's highest creatures, is presented in three scandalized words: 'Humans (*'āḏām*) kiss calves!'

Earlier in the book (6:4) God had likened the goodness of Ephraim and Judah to 'a morning cloud'[1] and to the short-lived dew of dawn. Now he presses the point right home – for a nation *is* no more than its morals and its character. So not only their shallow resolves, but 'they' themselves, will simply vanish from the scene. What is said of them is said elsewhere of individual sinners ('like the chaff', Ps. 1:4) and of all enemies of God (like 'smoke', Ps. 68:2).

No tame divinity

13:4 *I am the Lord your God*
        from the land of Egypt;
    you know no God but me,
        and besides me there is no saviour.
  5 *It was I who knew you in the wilderness,*
        in the land of drought;
  6 *but when they had fed to the full,*
        they were filled, and their heart was lifted up;
        therefore they forgot me.
  7 *So I will be to them like a lion,*
        like a leopard I will lurk beside the way.
  8 *I will fall upon them like a bear robbed of her cubs,*
        I will tear open their breast,
    and there I will devour them like a lion,
        as a wild beast would rend them.

Nothing could be further than the two halves of this paragraph from the popular picture of God as a tolerant spectator. First

---

[1] Or 'mist', as here. The Heb. of 6:4b is exactly echoed in our verse 3a.

He insists on fully personal relations ('you [shall]² *know* ...'; '... It was I who *knew* you ...') and on exclusive loyalty; then, for the breach of this, threatens to turn from saviour (4) into predator. In terms of the Ten Commandments, whose opening declaration seems to underlie these verses (see verse 4a), He is 'a jealous God'; and these threats of carnage make no apologies for the fact.

It need hardly be said that the childishness that makes up most of human jealousy has no place in God: only a fiery concern for what is precious to Him. It is as far from our 'envy, hatred and malice' as it is from cool indifference. Equally, there is nothing arbitrary in His judgments, excessive though they will often seem to us, and as uninhibited as in the ferocious picture of verse 8. The rest of the book must be allowed to put to us the other side of it, showing us not only the logic of our spiritual sowing and reaping (*e.g.* 8:7, 'the wind ... the whirl-wind'; 10:13, 'the fruit of lies'), our deafness to reason and appeal (8:12; 11:2), our obstinacy (4:16; 11:7), evasiveness (7:13) and wantonness (5:4), but supremely the deep reluctance of God to resort to judgment (11:8), and His longing that at last it may bring His people to their senses (5:13–15; chapter 14).

Who can help you?

13:9 *I will destroy you, O Israel;*
  who can help you?
  10 *Where now is your king, to save you;*
    where are all your princes, to defend you –
  those of whom you said,
    'Give me a king and princes'?
  11 *I have given you kings in my anger,*
    and I have taken them away in my wrath.

  12 *The iniquity of Ephraim is bound up,*
    his sin is kept in store.
  13 *The pangs of childbirth come for him,*
    but he is an unwise son;

---

² RSV's present tense, 'you know ...', is not the most obvious translation, and it breaks the implied link with the first commandment, whose statement 'I am the Lord' leads to the series of demands ('you shall ...') which are all expressed in the Heb. tense that we have here. AV, RV, NIV rightly translate it as a future.

for now he does not present himself
at the mouth of the womb.

The mood in which Israel had demanded a king is quite familiar to us: a compound of reasonable grievances (against misrule by Samuel's sons, 1 Sa. 8:1–5), ideas of grandeur ('like all the nations') and trust in the seen rather than the unseen ('that our king may ... go out before us and fight our battles', 1 Sa. 8:20).

Yet God made room for kingship and put it to noble use, as He still does with our bright ideas – or in spite of them. What He could not bless was the arrogance that gave rise to it and the power-struggles that exploited it. We have already seen its corruption in Hosea's day (7:3–7), and the utter disillusion that marked its downfall (10:3: 'a king, what could he do for us?'). The process by which God took these kings 'away in (His) wrath' was of their own choosing: a string of assassinations and coups from within, and the punitive might of Assyria from without, in reprisal for repeated acts of treachery.[3]

Hosea's wealth of imagery, perhaps unequalled among the prophets, is drawn on once again in verses 12 and 13 for a double thrust at Israelite complacency: first by picturing unforgiven sin as a well-kept store of trouble for the future, and then by the analogy of a birth that threatens to go fatally wrong. This second picture combines the tantalizing thought of early promise that has come to nothing, with that of a disaster that no-one can now avert. King Hezekiah of Judah would one day use this very metaphor, not in blank despair but in desperate appeal to God, and be answered by a miracle (2 Ki. 19:3ff.). In the northern kingdom there was no leader of that calibre or that faith.

The last enemy

13:14 *I will ransom them from the power of the grave;*
I will redeem them from death.
Where, O death, are your plagues?
Where, O grave, is your destruction?

I will have no compassion (NIV).

[3] 2 Ki. 15:8 – 17:6. See also the last six names of kings of Israel, and what befell them, on pp. 132ff.

Is this a ringing challenge to 'the last enemy', signalling his doom, or is it (as some would urge) nothing but the last nail in Israel's coffin? The NIV translation, above, agreeing with the New Testament (1 Cor. 15:54f.) and with the older versions as far back as the pre-Christian LXX, takes it as a great affirmation, one of the greatest in Scripture. That is, it treats the opening couplet of this verse as a straight promise, exactly as it is written; a promise to be unfolded by our Lord's great 'ransom' saying in Mark 10:45. Sadly, the modern trend is to turn it into a question expecting the answer No, and thereby to make the rest of the verse merely a call for the weapons of death to do their worst against Israel.[4]

So it needs to be pointed out that the Hebrew of 14a does *not* use the interrogative prefix, but has the form of a plain statement. Sometimes, to be sure, the context of a verse compels us to read a statement ironically or with an interrogative inflexion (see the footnote on 4:16b, p. 56), and this is why the present verse has suffered this treatment in some recent versions, for the surrounding gloom is certainly profound.

But what has been forgotten is that one of the outstanding features of this book is its sudden changes of tone from the sternest of threats to the warmest of resolves – most famously in 11:8,

> How can I give you up, O Ephraim!
> How can I hand you over, O Israel!
> . . . My heart recoils within me . . .

or in, *e.g.*, 1:9–10,

> Call his name Not my people . . .
> Yet . . . it shall be said to them,
> "Sons of the living God."

Indeed the over-all structure of the prophecy leads through judgment into the 'broad, sunlit uplands' of the final chapter, just as in fact the disastrous history of Israel and Judah turned out to be the prelude to the very destruction of death that is

---

[4] This is the point of RSV, JB, made doubly explicit in NEB: 'Oh, for your plagues, O death!' (*etc.*), and in GNB, 'Bring on your plagues, death!' (*etc.*).

promised here.[5] The 'compassion' which God withholds in the final line is, of course, withheld not from the victims of death and the grave, but from this pair of tyrants themselves. *Cf.* the personifying of them in Revelation 20:14, 'Then Death and Hades were thrown into the lake of fire.' In less pictorial terms, God promises the utter end of death and its dominion, with no question of His modifying that resolve.[6]

No quarter for Samaria

13:15 *Though he may flourish as the reed plant,*
    the east wind, the wind of the Lord, shall come,
    rising from the wilderness;
  and his fountain shall dry up,
    his spring shall be parched;
  it shall strip his treasury
    of every precious thing.
  16 *Samaria shall bear her guilt,*
    because she has rebelled against her God;
  they shall fall by the sword,
    their little ones shall be dashed in pieces,
    and their pregnant women ripped open.

The name Ephraim had the attractive sound of 'flourishing' (15a), and had been chosen for that reason: 'For God', said Joseph, 'has made me fruitful in the land of my affliction' (Gn. 41:52). In comparison with Judah and some of her southern cousins,[7] the northern kingdom of Ephraim/Israel was fertile, and had recently been very prosperous. But, in common with all material prosperity, Ephraim's wealth was as vulnerable to an aggressor as an orchard to an east wind.

And what an aggressor! Assyria was noted for its cruelty in war, and would certainly not stop short of the atrocities which

[5] A further detail in 14b, confirming the nature of the verse as a taunt against the last enemy, is that our Heb. text has 'I will be (*'hy*) your plagues, O death; I will be (*'hy*) your destruction, O Sheol'. LXX evidently used a text which had *'yh* ('Where?') at the points where MT has *'hy* ('I will be'). The difference only becomes a major one when the text is reinterpreted with RSV, NEB, *etc.*

[6] Another interpretation of this final line, however, is that it introduces the next oracle (15f.), as NIV suggests by its spacing and punctuation.

[7] The Heb. text of 15a has '. . . flourish among brothers', which hardly needs the emendation to 'as the reed plant'.

119

lesser powers allowed themselves. There is a sickening frequency of references to the butchery described in 16b: see the list in the footnote to 10:14b (p. 99).

So the prophet refuses to soften his warning by clothing it in abstract terms. The fate that his people were bringing on themselves would be all too sharp and physical, pressed home in revolting detail. But mercifully, although it would mean the end of all that they had promised themselves, it was not the last word from God.

Hosea 14:1–9
The way home

This little chapter of only nine verses,[1] as quiet and gentle as its predecessors were tumultuous, leads us back again through the main areas of the book, this time on our way home. Israel is being beckoned, and the way is signposted with the landmarks which she passed on her spiritual journey into the far country.

Draw near to God . . .

14:1 *Return, O Israel, to the Lord your God,*
        for you have stumbled because of your iniquity.
   2 *Take with you words*
        and return to the Lord;
      say to him,
           'Take away all iniquity;
      accept that which is good
        and we will render
        the fruit of our lips.
   3 *Assyria shall not save us,*
        we will not ride upon horses;
      and we will say no more, "Our God,"
        to the work of our hands.
      In thee the orphan finds mercy.'

The first word, 'Return', is an old friend, a strong feature of the book. Up to now it has brought only disappointment and

---

[1] The Heb. Bible has ten verses, through starting the chapter at 13:16; so its numbering runs one verse ahead of the English versions throughout the chapter.

reproach. Basically it means 'turn'; and Israel has habitually turned the wrong way. They have been 'bent on turning away from me', as 11:7 puts it. This, incidentally, was obscured by the older translations that spoke of 'backsliding', which has a sound of failure rather than perversity, whereas in fact there had been a flat refusal to respond (11:5), born of pride (7:10) and of settled preference ('their deeds do not permit them to return to their God', 5:4). Any response to the great call, 'Come, let us return to the Lord . . .', had so far been as shallow as a passing impulse (6:1, 4).

But God will not give up – how could He?[2] If their repentance has been shallow, He will deepen it. There is warmth in the emphatic form of the word 'return' here (1a; verse 2 uses the ordinary form), and the preposition is a strong one.[3] We could almost translate it, '*Oh turn, Israel, right back to the Lord.*' Even the familiar words, 'your God', have gained a new intensity from the threat which Israel's fickleness had seemed to pose to her marriage-bond with the Lord. Against all deserving, the marriage holds; He is still hers. Here is the costly equivalent of His word to the cuckolded Hosea: 'Go again, love a woman who is beloved of a paramour . . .; even as the Lord loves the people of Israel, though they turn to other gods' (3:1).

Repentance, then, will have to start with the matter of the broken loyalty. 'I will allure her . . . and . . . she shall answer as in the days of her youth' (2:14f.). As George Adam Smith finely puts it, 'Amos cries, "Turn, for in front of you is destruction;" but Hosea, "Turn, for behind you is God." '[4]

For all its warmth, though, God's calling is exacting. It leaves no room for humbug: there must be 'fruit that befits repentance'. Already chapter 12:6 has held up to us the challenging implications of this. Manward, it will mean 'Hold fast to love and justice'; and heavenward, 'Wait continually for your God.' It is the second of these that our chapter will be chiefly spelling out.

First, then, 'Take with you *words*' (verse 2). Words can be facile, but so can actions. A major contrast in this book is between articulate, meaningful encounter and the mere

[2] *Cf.* 11:8–9.   [3] *Cf.* BDB, p. 724a, citing this verse (14:2, Heb.).
[4] Smith, p. 339.

formalities and offerings which people try to substitute for it. 'With their flocks and herds they shall go to seek the Lord, but they will not find him' (5:6). Sub-personal religion never will (*cf.* 5:15).

These 'words' are to be without reservations or excuses. God has spoken of 'your iniquity' (verse 1); man must accept and echo that (verse 2), not jib at it or play it down as he did in 12:8 with his boast, 'they shall find in me none iniquity that were sin' (RV).

But what of the next plea, 'Accept that which is good'? The AV, perhaps scenting salvation by works, gave the rather forced translation, 'Receive (us) graciously.' G. A. F. Knight mentions another just-possible rendering, 'Receive (us), O Good One.' But more probably it is simply a plea that God will accept the offering from the lips and the heart which He has required of His people. This chimes in with the famous saying in 6:6 about the things which He desires above sacrifice, and with Psalm 51:17; perhaps, too, with the verbal echo, obscured in translation, between God's call, 'Take with you ...', and man's response, 'Accept (lit. 'take') ...'.

The offering of words, which began with one kind of confession, the acknowledgment of sin, now turns into confession in its other sense, the acknowledgment of God in praise. The Hebrew of verse 2c is awkward again: literally, 'and we will render bullocks, our lips'; but at least the word 'render' gives a good clue to the sense. It is the term used for paying one's vows (*e.g.* Ps. 116:14) in due gratitude for answered prayer. Lips, then, will be our votive offering, our sacrificial 'bullocks'. But the point is made more gracefully in the Greek and Syriac versions, which read the same consonants to mean 'the fruit of our lips', and this is how Hebrews 13:15 quotes it.

So far, then, the positive side of repentance has been uppermost. The runaway must return, the sinner plead, the formalist use his mind and lips, to come back into fellowship with God. It is a turning to the light.

Now with verse 3 comes the negative requirement, a turning *from* the old ways, in a clear farewell to futile hopes and false beliefs. Both are familiar from the earlier chapters. For security, Israel has been playing a double game, banking on Assyria at one moment, and on Egypt (that source of horses and chariots, 3a; *cf.* Is. 31:1) the next. We have seen those two

names in almost every chapter since the middle of the book –
for Israel was as loth as we are to play these matters straight, or
to take God seriously. *His* name carried no weight in politics.

As for false beliefs, the gods of verse 3b are constantly in
evidence throughout the book. Hosea's scorn for them is as
total as Israel's infatuation. No doubt our own scorn echoes
his. But as long as 'the work of our hands' looms larger to us
than the One who made these hands, verse 3b will still have
words for us to use.

The trustful climax of the confession is beautifully, if freely,
expressed in NEB: 'for in thee the fatherless finds a father's love'
– which brings out the allusion in the Hebrew to the way the
book began, with the prophet's broken marriage and disowned
daughter, Lo-ruhamah, which means virtually 'Unloved' (1:6).
For Lo-ruhamah was to be re-named Ruhamah, 'She is loved'
(2:1, 23),[5] in token of the Lord's reclaiming grace for Israel.
Once again this chapter has taken up the opening themes of the
book, filling them with hope.

. . . and he will draw near to you

14:4 *I will heal their faithlessness;*
 I will love them freely,
 for my anger has turned from them.
 5 *I will be as the dew to Israel;*
 he shall blossom as the lily,
 he shall strike root as the poplar,
 6 *his shoots shall spread out;*
 his beauty shall be like the olive,
 and his fragrance like Lebanon.
 7 *They shall return and dwell beneath my shadow,*
 they shall flourish as a garden;
 they shall blossom as the vine,
 their fragrance shall be like the wine of Lebanon.

Now God speaks, and the whole scene lights up before us. The
word '(Re)turn' still echoes through the chapter, as it has
echoed through the whole book. It was heard in verses 1 and 2,

---

[5] The verb which RSV translates here in terms of 'mercy', and in chapters 1
and 2 in terms of 'pity', is also translated 'love' in Ps. 18:1 (2, Heb.).

and will reappear in verse 7; meanwhile it comes twice in verse 4, first concealed in the word 'faithlessness' (lit. 'turning'; *i.e.*, 'apostasy', NEB), to remind us that our waywardness is incurable until God heals it; and then in the assurance of the last line that His anger has 'turned' away. Between these two reminders of the past comes one of the purest expressions of what the New Testament will call grace, prevailing over the language of judgment and desert heard in 9:15 ('I will love them no more'). The NEB translates our present line, 'Of my own bounty will I love them.' We can notice, too, a telling contrast, not only between this outgoing love and the scant affection of Israel's paramours (2:7), but between this tireless Giver and the reluctant hirelings of 8:8–9.

After the perfect clarity of these promises – and clarity is vital to the anxious and conscience-stricken – the poetry is free to spread itself in the next verses (5–7). All the imagery of them is from nature, at its happiest and most bountiful.

Without labouring the details, we can gain from this a threefold impression of Israel revived and reconciled to God. First, freshness (dew, flowers, fragrance, beauty, shade); secondly, stability (rooted like the poplar, perhaps; or like Lebanon; verse 5[6]); thirdly, vigour (the spreading shoots of new growth, verse 6; the 'corn in abundance', verse 7, NEB).[7]

But such a summary is useful only if it makes us look more closely at the passage, which has all the grace and vitality to match the realities of which it speaks. There is nothing stifling or constricting in the divine love expressed here. Like the river of Ezekiel 47, it brings life to everything it reaches.

The appeal pressed home

14:8 O *Ephraim, what have I to do with idols?*
   It is I who answer and look after you.

---

[6] Most modern versions reckon the 'Lebanon', the final word of each of the next two verses (6 and 7, or in the Heb. Bible 7 and 8), has induced a scribal error in verse 5, where they conjecture that *libneh* (poplar) stood originally. But the Heb. text is supported by the ancient versions in ending all three verses with 'Lebanon', which is not only poetically effective but, in verse 5, is perfectly intelligible, as referring either to its mountain range or (NIV) to its cedars.

[7] See RSV mg. The Heb. text has 'they shall make corn (*dāgān*) flourish' (lit. 'live'), which RSV has emended to 'they shall flourish as a garden' (*gan*).

I am like an evergreen cypress,
from me comes your fruit.

'*O Ephraim!*' Such an exclamation has more than once already
laid bare the heart of the prophecy and of its ultimate Author.
Like David's cry, 'O my son Absalom!' (2 Sa. 18:33) or our
Lord's 'O Jerusalem, Jerusalem!' (Mt. 23:37), it has voiced
both love and anguish: 'What shall I do with you, O Ephraim?'
'How can I give you up, O Ephraim!' (6:4; 11:8). Now (as I see
it) it is as though God turns to reason with the hearer for the last
time – for the penitent words of verses 2 and 3 and the fair
prospect of verses 4–7 were part of an invitation (verses 1, 2a)
which has yet to be accepted and made Israel's own.

The plea (on this view)[8] rests on the incomparable claims of
God. Can He any longer[9] be spoken of, even thought of, in the
same breath as idols? Can Egypt's or Assyria's protection
compete with His? Do they answer when you call? Do they
care as He cares?

The last two lines of this verse read strangely until we remember that Hebrew thought has none of our inhibitions
against mixed metaphors. God, these lines can well be saying,
has all the constancy of the evergreen, all the richness of the
fruit tree. Ephraim, if he is to live up to his own name ('For God
has made me fruitful . . .', Gn. 41:52), need look no further.

Epilogue: To the reader . . .

14:9 *Whoever is wise, let him understand these things;*
    whoever is discerning, let him know them;
 for the ways of the Lord are right,
    and the upright walk in them,
    but transgressors stumble in them.

---

[8] The English versions reflect something of the variety of possible interpretations. In the first line, JB, GNB and NEB ('What has Ephraim to do with idols any
more?') make use of LXX. In AV, RV, Ephraim is the speaker. In the last two lines,
opinions differ as to the identity of the speaker or speakers; it has even been
suggested that in the four lines of the verse, God and Ephraim speak alternately
(Pusey).

[9] RSV eases the question by omitting 'any longer'. But the note of time is
intelligible if it refers to the effect of the prophecy on the hearers' understanding.

Whether the prophet himself or an editor added these words need hardly concern us here. The point they drive home is that the prophecy is open-ended: its eloquence and passion could win Israel to repentance or could leave her unmoved. The response was hers to make.

But not only hers. The '*whoever*' of this verse suddenly exposes us to the same searching encounter, for the word of God goes on speaking; it never slips safely into the past. The rightness of God's ways as revealed in this book is so far above us in both holiness and love, as to leave self-sufficient man without excuse, self-condemned, while those who turn into the way of righteousness find themselves met more than halfway.

> To turn aside from thee is hell,
> To walk with thee is heaven.

The comment of G. A. F. Knight on this verse deserves to be the last word:

> 'Therefore, dear reader, so runs the content of this Epilogue, ask yourself the question – how would you apply this message of Hosea to your own knowledge and experience of Israel's God?'

Addenda

Maps
Chronological table
A bird's-eye view of the book

THE BREAK-UP OF ISRAEL

Between 734 and 722 BC the kingdom of Israel and most of its northern neighbours were reduced to petty provinces of the Assyrian empire.

In 734/3, Galilee, Gilead and the coastal strip were taken (2 Ki. 15:29; Is. 9:1), to become the provinces of Megiddo, Gilead and Dor.

Finally, 724-722, Samaria was besieged and taken, and its king replaced by an imperial governor. The new provinces were depopulated, to be resettled with peoples from distant parts of the empire (2 Ki. 17:24-41).

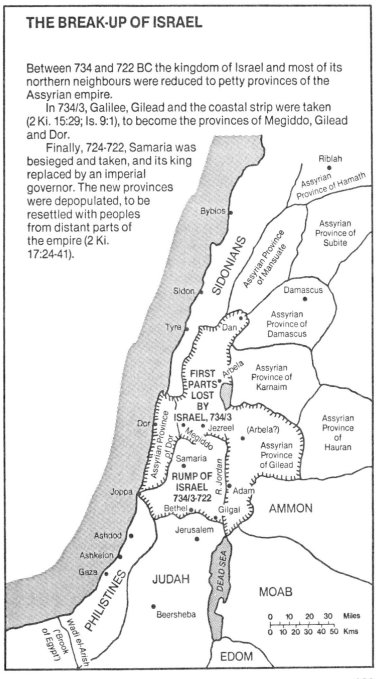

129

The kingdoms of Judah (the south) and Israel (the north) from the death of Solomon to the fall of Samaria

Kings of Judah	(Prophets)	Kings of Israel
931 Rehoboam		931 Jeroboam I
913 Abijam		
911 Asa		910 Nadab, killed by
		↙
		909 Baasha
		886 Elah, killed by
		↙
		885 Zimri: suicide, on defeat by
		↙
		885 Omri
870 Jehoshaphat (father's co-regent from 873) (see footnote on co-regency p. 134)	(Elijah)	874 **Ahab**
		853 Ahaziah
848 Jehoram (father's co-regent from 853)	(Elisha)	852 Jehoram, killed by ↙
841 Ahaziah, killed by →		841 **Jehu**
841 Queen Athaliah		

Assyrian aggression against Israel and her neighbours

Kings of Assyria

Assyrian campaigns reach Lebanon and the coast of Philistia, terrorizing and extorting tribute.

Ashur-nasir-pal II
883–859

853   Westward drive halted at the battle of Qarqar, by a coalition headed by Syria and Israel. King **Ahab** supplied 2,000 chariots and 14,000 men, according to the Assyrian records.

Shalmaneser III
859–824

841   Assyrians besiege Damascus and its king Hazael, then storm round Palestine, exacting tribute from (among others) King **Jehu** of Israel.

Shalmaneser III
859–824

131

Kings of Judah	(Prophets)	Kings of Israel
835 Joash		
		814 Jehoahaz
796 Amaziah		798 Joash
767 **Uzziah** (Azariah) (father's co-regent from 791)	(Jonah)	782 **Jeroboam II** (father's co-regent from 793)
	(Amos) **(Hosea)**	
		753 **Zechariah**, killed by ↙
		752 **Shallum**, killed by ↙
		752 **Menahem**
		742 **Pekahiah**, killed by ↙
740 **Jotham** (father's co-regent from 750)	(Isaiah) (Micah)	740 **Pekah**, killed by
732 **Ahaz** (father's co-regent from 744)		732 **Hoshea**

132

Kings of Assyria

804–802	Assyria crushes Damascus. Israel, long harassed by Hazael of Damascus, now enters a half-century of peace and affluence.	Adad-nirari III 810–781

Tiglath-pileser III, 745–727

Menahem had reigned as Tiglath-pileser's vassal, but *c.* 735 King **Pekah** conspires with Damascus, Gaza, *etc.*, against Assyria.

734–732	Assyria sweeps down the Philistine coast, truncates Israel (see map) and takes Damascus. But **Hoshea** assassinates Pekah and submits to Assyria to preserve what is left of Israel.	Tiglath-pileser III, 745–727

133

Kings of Judah   **Kings of Israel**

                                  722 THE FALL OF
                                  SAMARIA
                                  (the end of the
                                  northern kingdom)

715 Hezekiah
    (father's co-regent
    from 729)

[1] The practice of co-regency (evidenced by the overlapping dates of certain kings) was presumably a precaution against disputes over the succession, as well as a means of giving the crown prince experience of government. Note Judah's stable dynasty, the house of David, in contrast to Israel's many coups and changes.

Kings of Assyria

Hoshea now plots with Egypt against
Assyria. Shalmaneser has him seized, and
724– invades Israel. The capital, Samaria, holds
722 out from 724 to 722, then falls to Sargon II,
Shalmaneser's successor. Israel's inhabitants
are deported, to be replaced by other subject
peoples.

Shalmaneser V
727–722

Sargon II
722–705

A bird's-eye view of the book

subject. She has left me, says God, for what her lovers promised her: all the fertile wealth of nature. She little knew that I myself, not her new gods, was the giver of it all!

So I will stop the flow, till she has nothing left but shame. Then I will court her again, and at last she will respond. This time it will be for ever. It will be like paradise regained; and the whole family will be at one.

3:1–5　'Love . . . as the Lord loves'　39

Now Hosea is sent to win back his own fickle wife, with love like the Lord's love. He has to buy her back – such is her new friend. Then he makes it clear that, from now on, no-one must come between them.

So too, after the discipline of long privation, a chastened Israel will at last come truly home.

Part Two: Hosea 4–14　The parable spelt out　45

'HOW CAN I GIVE YOU UP?'

4:1–19　A people without understanding　46

Israel! You are a moral jungle! I charge you with every sin in the book. But you, sir priest, are the true villain. You, the teacher, have no use for knowledge, when knowledge could have saved my people. So I have no use for you. You and your flock will take your punishment together.

Can this be my people? Pagan and

promiscuous, stubborn and sodden, you are fit for neither man nor God: only to be left to your own devices.

| 5:1–14 | The prospect darkens | 56 |

Priests, people, king! I find you as treacherous as a trap, as tainted as a harlot. You may think that you can choose your moment to repent, and can buy your way back into favour. But your sins are too strong for you, and your God has withdrawn.

Yes, I myself will hasten your decay, and I am now your predator; so no power on earth can help you.

You must learn the hard way now.

| 5:15 – 7:2 | Let us press on to know the Lord | 62 |

When I am hard on you, and hard to find, it is to get you seeking. I must have your loyal love, not your fleeting piety or your sacrifices.

But what do I find? Nothing but disloyalty, nothing but violence, and not a flicker of concern.

| 7:3–16 | Decadence | 69 |

Will the king and court, guardians of justice, stem this tide of evil? But they wallow and revel in it, and their revelry is murderous.

The whole nation is in disarray and mortal danger; yet nothing will induce it to think, to pray, to repent, or even to be honest with me. Looking in every direction but mine, it has turned against the very one who brought it up from infancy.

When will they wake up to their danger and to my anger? How complacently they provoke me with their favourite devices – kings and gods of their own making; allies bought with promises; altars everywhere; and fortresses that will be death-traps.

The orgy is over. What looms up now is exile. Instead of bargaining with Egypt and Assyria you will be living there – as refugees in the one, as captives in the other. What will become of your fancy religion then? And of your mockery of my prophets?

All your early promise has failed, for it was never genuine. You have always hankered after pagan gods and pagan ways. Now you must have your fill of them.

When everything went well it was pagan altars, pagan symbols everywhere. Now that all this has failed, and worse is imminent, will you listen at last? There is still a moment left, still a choice of harvests, that the Lord 'may come and rain righteousness upon you'. But the harvest you are bringing on yourselves is butchery. Assyrian butchery – you remember what that was like, last time?

Do you think you mean as little to me as I mean to you? I was a father to you. I taught you to walk!

But you have turned against me, and you have made up your mind. You must go through with it now: with everything that you were warned against.

Yet how can I destroy you? My love remains, and in the end my sons will come back, shaken and ashamed, home to me again.

11:12 – 12:14   Look back and learn!   106

Look back now to Jacob, and see your crooked selves! But look on, too, to what God made of him when Jacob strove and wept and sought, not for advantage but for grace.

Then look at your complacent, affluent selves. You are no pilgrims! To you now only money talks – you have no ears for my prophets, who were once the making of you. You must get back to your beginnings; and if you must take your punishment you have only yourselves to blame.

13:1–16   The unmaking of a kingdom   113

Once more look back. See what you were, and what you have become. See what I did for you, and how you have repaid it.

Who will extricate you now? Not I – I am the predator! Not your king – he has been taken. True, the last enemy, death, shall not have the last word; yet your city must fall, and fall to the merciless.

14:1–9   The way home   120

Even now, dear Israel, turn right back to God! Attempt no payment: only seek frank forgiveness, and have done with earthly substitutes for your Lord.

And His reply? 'I will heal ..., I will love ...; they shall dwell beneath my shadow.' Where sin abounded, grace will much more abound.

So to the reader: all these things are words for everyman, not just for Israel. Here is your safe path; or here, if you insist, your downfall.